T0193911

SEQUINS
of HOPE

A Journey to New Life

ALLY BRYCE NEAL

WESTBOW
PRESS®
A DIVISION OF THOMAS NELSON
& ZONDERVAN

WestBow Press books may be ordered through booksellers or by contacting:

WestBow Press
A Division of Thomas Nelson & Zondervan
1663 Liberty Drive
Bloomington, IN 47403
www.westbowpress.com
1 (866) 928-1240

Unless otherwise noted scripture taken from the Holy Bible, New International Version. NIV. Copyright 1973, 1978, 1984 by International Bible Society. Used by permission of Zondervan. All rights reserved.

Scripture quotations marked NLT are taken from the Holy Bible, New Living Translation, copyright 1996, 2004, 2007. Used by permission of Tyndale House Publishers, Inc. Carol Stream, Illinois 60188. All rights reserved.

ISBN: 978-1-5127-8141-0 (sc)
ISBN: 978-1-5127-8142-7 (hc)
ISBN: 978-1-5127-8140-3 (e)

Library of Congress Control Number: 2017904808

Print information available on the last page.

WestBow Press rev. date: 04/21/2017

Jesus came to redeem and restore you to the truth of who you are, so take His hand and journey to a new life.

CONTENTS

Preface ix

Introduction xi

Chapter 1   The Journey Begins 1

Chapter 2   Nothing Is Impossible with God 14

Chapter 3   Garment of Praise for a Spirit of Despair 27

Chapter 4   What Are You Hoping For? 39

Chapter 5   By His Stripes 51

Chapter 6   Robe of Righteousness 61

Chapter 7   If Only I Believed 73

Chapter 8   Beauty from Ashes 83

Chapter 9   A White Flag Called Victory.......................................94

Chapter 10 Joy of the Redeemed 107

Chapter 11 Sequins of Hope 120

Works Cited 133

About the Author 135

PREFACE

If you have ever experienced hurt, this book is for you. This book includes Holy Spirit-inspired messages of hope, healing, and restoration that were given to me while I was serving as a minister of pastoral care. I used these messages as a ministry to the broken and to whosoever will. When the Lord shared that He wanted this to become a book, I included each message as the heart of the journey to new life. I have kept the work the same and added the interwoven words of the journey.

You can tell a person repeatedly who he or she is in Christ, but until he or she believes it, he or she will not get it. Jesus came "to proclaim freedom for the captives and release from darkness for the prisoners" (Isa. 61:1). Through my personal journey and revelation of God's healing power, God taught me the key to receiving the truth within our hearts of who we truly are in Christ. My desire is to share this revelation with you. Are you ready to journey to a new life with me? If so, you will never be the same. The key ingredient in this journey to restoration and healing is the moving of God's truth from head knowledge to heart knowledge.

This book is one of hope and comfort. God is sovereign over every single detail of your life. He is with you. While I will share certain truths on healing that I personally experienced in my journey, these serve as a frame of reference on how restoration may happen. God will lead you into all truths about your particular journey. My goal is to take you to the one, Jesus, who is able to meet you where you are. Jesus is your only hope, healer, restorer, and redeemer. My goal is to release you to Him, the one who is mighty to save! Are you ready to start your journey to a new life?

INTRODUCTION

There is something about the night in the city of Charleston, South Carolina that is different. It seems the city comes alive as tourists walk the streets, enjoying the fine dining restaurants. On a hot summer night, your senses come alive as you catch a southern breeze from a gently swaying palm tree. There is no place like it. The lights seem to shine brighter, and even in the darkness, there is such beauty. For me, this journey has had many contrasts of light and darkness, of hope and hopelessness. It is my desire that you will be touched by these words and realize that, even in darkness, there is a great light.

This book is written for whosoever seeks hope in the dark and broken places. I don't know what you may be going through or what you went through, but I do know the one who wants to redeem all of it, to give you a fresh start, a new life.

As I prepare to submit this book for publishing, I wonder if the ones who will purchase this book will be searching for hope. Will they be saying those words, "The destruction is so great in my life"? And so I wonder if my journey—my broken heart—can make a difference in others' lives. God is a God of redemption. He always redeems what is broken. He promises in scripture time after time the redemption of His people. Will you journey with me to a new life? Like the sequins on a fine garment, will you open your heart to the hope that awaits you in the pages of this book?

Jesus came to redeem and to restore, to give back all that has been taken in life's journey. He is alive today, and He is our only source of hope. The work of Jesus and His blood shed on the cross brings healing and restoration to our lives. Through Jesus's work on the cross, we are returned to relationship with God. My prayer is that whosoever reads this book will receive a revelation (to believe and know) of who they are in Christ, and from this revelation, they will walk in restoration and freedom.

We worship a sovereign and powerful God who always does more than we can ever ask or imagine. I am a testimony that "all things work together for those who love the Lord" (Rom. 8:28 NIV).

Hope is eternal. It is not a feeling. It doesn't fade or rust. It's eternal! Thank you for allowing me to speak into your life. It is no accident that each of you chose this book. And what the enemy came to destroy or what has been taken or lost, Jesus came to give back. "The thief comes only to steal and kill and destroy; I have come that they may have life, and have it to the full. I am the good shepherd. The good shepherd lays down his life for the sheep" (John 10:10–11).

I pray that the Savior will touch you as you read the pages of this book and that you will realize how much God loves you. While these are just words on a page, I pray that, just as these words have touched lives in the past, these messages will touch your life. As we move along, I often repeat certain points more than once because, through repetition, I believe the truth starts to sink in. So please forgive me for repeating myself. My hope is to release you to Jesus, who promises to never leave nor forsake you. He will walk with you through your suffering. And finally my prayer is that you will take His hand and walk with Him, having Him lead you each day and step of your pain and life.

First, let me say that you are each daughters and sons of the King. God loves you so much! He redeems the brokenness of our lives and wants to heal your heart. He healed—and continues to heal—mine. We all have a story. And guess what? God cares about our story and our lives. He is able and wants to walk with you in your pain. None of us is exempt from pain. Sometimes it may only be at this place that we can choose to fully surrender to Christ. If your brokenness is due to another person's sin, it is important to remember that it is not your fault if another person hurts you. God wants to restore you as the daughter and son that you are!

I am here to testify that God is a God who is in the business of healing and restoring our brokenness. He wants to and is able to meet you where you are. God promises to exchange your ashes for beauty, your spirit of heaviness with the oil of joy, your mourning with comfort, your broken heart with healing, your captivity with freedom, and your spirit of despair with a garment of praise. God does that with our lives. He gives us a second chance. He always redeems what is broken. "For God so loved the world that he gave his one and only Son, that whoever believes in him shall not perish but have eternal life" (John 3:16).

Isaiah 52:7–9 says,

> How beautiful on the mountains are the feet of those who bring good news, who proclaim peace, who bring good tidings, who proclaim salvation, who say to Zion, "Your God reigns!" Listen! Your watchmen lift up their voices; together they shout for joy. When the LORD returns to Zion, they will see it with their own eyes. Burst into songs of joy together, you ruins of Jerusalem, for the LORD has comforted his people, he has redeemed Jerusalem.

Jesus came "to proclaim freedom for the captives and release from darkness for the prisoners" (Isa. 61:1). Through my personal journey and a revelation of God's healing power, He revealed the key to receiving the truth of who we are in Christ. My desire is to share this revelation with others. I believe that you can tell a person repeatedly who he or she is in Christ, but until he or she believes it in his or her heart, it will only be head knowledge.

The chapters of this book will carry you through this journey to new life. Are you ready to journey with me to new life? If so, you will never be the same!

As we journey to new life, we will also receive revelations of God's grace, His comfort, and His strength, but we will ultimately receive a revelation of His Hope. In my journey, I had difficulty in finding the joy, and in fact, it took a long time for me to find the joy. I didn't locate it until the end of these messages. It is my hope that, as you read, you will recognize the joy all throughout the journey because the joy never disappears. There are beautiful sparkles of joy in the journey.

This book, like a fine diamond, is multifaceted. While it is a great read, there is freedom for others who might go deeper and use this as an additional resource or learning tool. The last chapter of this book can also serve as a leader's guide for group study. In addition, because the original messages of hope and restoration are included in the text, these messages within this book could be shared as messages of hope and restoration within a ministry group setting.

Remember that the healing and restoration process is as multifaceted as a diamond. And I must add that a diamond is only so beautiful because of the refining process.

CHAPTER 1

The Journey Begins

It was a beautiful afternoon as I stopped at a local grocer on the way to the beach. As I parked my car, I noticed two ladies admiring shirts, which it appeared that the other had recently purchased. One of the absolutely gorgeous shirts caught my eye. The white shirt had the word "joy" on it in gold, sparkly letters.

As she held it up, her friend asked, "Where did you get that?"

The six words "where did you get that" and "joy" took me back in my memory. I remembered something at that moment. I found my joy on the beach of Isle of Palms as I shared all of the hurt, pain, heartache, anger, and devastation of my journey. I sensed the Lord affirming His promises that He was with me the entire time, every minute, and would use all of it to help others. "Praise be to the God and Father of our Lord Jesus Christ, the Father of compassion and the God of all comfort, who comforts us in all our troubles, so that we can comfort those in any trouble with the comfort we ourselves receive from God" (II Corinthians 1:3-4). I felt a joy in my heart that I have never experienced before. I felt the love of the Father for me, even in the suffering. I finally got it that God cared and He had been there all along.

I realized that, while I did not notice the beautiful sparkles of joy during my journey, it did not take away from the fact that the joy was always there. I was just looking for it in the wrong place. I was searching for it in my circumstances. I was desiring for life to be a certain way, and if it weren't, I had no joy.

Isle of Palms is a beautiful beach that is constantly changing. It always looks different each time I visit the area. But one thing that is constant is the sparkles of silver throughout the sand. Do I notice the sparkles every time I visit that beach? No! But this does not change the fact that the sparkles are always there.

The same is said for joy. Though life circumstances can leave us feeling no joy, I have learned that it doesn't change the fact that joy is promised to us as believers. God has promised to never leave us or forsake us. He is near to the brokenhearted. But you see that this can be a journey because deep pain, hurt, and suffering can leave us focusing on the loss and the hurt and not the healer, deliverer, redeemer, or restorer. My prayer is that my shared journey will help you to see that Jesus is with you every single step of the journey and you won't miss the sparkles of joy all around you because you will see His hand with you, holding and healing you.

A journey is a process. Just as a butterfly has a morphing process, so too do we. Our wing may be broken, the wind may be knocked out of us, and we may feel shattered and broken. That is when we need to take Jesus's hand and share all of it—everything—with Him. Let the light of Jesus shine on your brokenness, and you will soon be soaring like a beautiful butterfly.

I am still drawn to the beauty of those three letters, joy. The woman's next shirt was white with a green turtle and the words "Merry Christmas" on it. Turtle was so appropriate for Isle of Palms, the place where I had found my joy. However, look at the word "joy," as in "Joy to the world! The Lord has come." How appropriate for the moment. Jesus is our only joy and only hope. Don't wait for the joy as I did. It is always with us.

I knew this book had sparkles of joy and hope all over it. While this is a journey to new life, it has sparkles of joy throughout. Although I had to search for it, I found it one day while walking on the beach of Isle of Palms, sharing in retrospect all of the pain and heartache I had experienced. And so these messages are Holy Spirit-inspired words of hope, healing, and restoration. They were given to me to be shared with others who are in dark times. They are a journey of hope that never gave up, of healing and of restoration. My prayer is that they will bless you and draw you to the only one who can deliver and give freedom. Reach out your hand. He is waiting to take it as you journey to a new life.

This journey is a metaphor for the process. Your entire life is a journey and in every detail of it, including the suffering, God is sovereign and will use it for good. All of the bad is part of the process of your journey and God can redeem it all. Every moment of our life counts toward what God is doing in our life. God can redeem even our mistakes. In my personal journey, I have experienced several times of brokenness. There are times in my journey where I was left sitting in the midst of shock, shattered dreams, disbelief, fear, and a desire to turn back the clock. A thousand questions filled me. My world was spinning. These were times of great growth opportunity for me. While I did not see it at the time, in retrospect these times are what brought me the most healing and the opportunity to share that with others like you. My prayer is that, as you read my journey, you will relate and begin to put back together the pieces of your life. I hope this is one book that you will want to read over and over because you will receive hope from it. I believe its messages are meant to provide hope and light in dark times. Ultimately, this book is a catalyst. I am carrying you to Jesus and releasing you to take His hand and walk in relationship with Him to restoration.

We all have a story. And guess what? God cares about our story and our lives. While I don't know what the enemy may have come to take from you, I do know that no one is immune from suffering. You have suffered. You will suffer. You will know someone who is suffering or will. Suffering is a part of life in a fallen world. Sometimes it is only at this place where we can learn to choose to fully surrender to Christ. If your brokenness is due to another person's sin, it is important to remember that it is not your fault if another person hurts you. God wants to restore you as the daughter or son that you are!

Isaiah 35 is a beautiful reflection of what God does when He enters the scene. Imagine with me, if you will. You are in a desert with everything seeming to be lifeless. Isn't this just how we feel when we experience a traumatic experience, loss, or other painful situation? We feel alone and empty, and it seems no one understands our pain. Life goes on around us, but we are merely walking around as if watching it, yet not connected. All seems lost. There seems to be no color or joy. There's just darkness.

God always uses the backdrop of restoration. In the painful experiences of our lives, He is setting up the backdrop of our lives with beauty, joy, and hope. And so one day God will restore all things. He will restore and provide justice for all of the wrong done to us and all of mankind throughout all of history. He loves to show His glory in His creation. You know what else? We see the light the brightest in the dark.

In Isaiah 35:1–10, we have a beautiful image of the desert blooming with new life. This is a metaphor of God's promises to bring restoration to the broken places of our lives. One of the most beautiful beaches I have ever visited was in Saint Martin, an island located in the Caribbean. One thing that I will always remember about that vacation was the beautiful, fragrant flowers that bloomed so close to the sandy beaches. It was such a beautiful contrast: the sand that would appear not able to sustain life and the beautiful flowers that often served as hedges between the beach and the grounds. It was breathtaking. To me, as I reflect back, this beautiful combination of the sand, water, and flowers, which appealed to all of my senses, defines my landscape of new life.

> The desert and the parched land will be glad; the wilderness will rejoice and blossom. Like the crocus, it will burst into bloom; it will rejoice greatly and shout for joy. The glory of Lebanon will be given to it, the splendor of Carmel and Sharon; they will see the glory of the LORD, the splendor of our God. Strengthen the feeble hands, steady the knees that give way; say to those with fearful hearts, "Be strong, do not fear; your God will come, he will come with vengeance; with divine retribution he will come to save you." Then will the eyes of the blind be opened and the ears of the deaf unstopped. Then will the lame leap like a deer, and the mute tongue shout for joy. Water will gush forth in the wilderness and streams in the desert. The burning

sand will become a pool, the thirsty ground bubbling springs. In the haunts where jackals once lay, grass and reeds and papyrus will grow. And a highway will be there; it will be called the Way of Holiness; it will be for those who walk on that Way. The unclean will not journey on it; wicked fools will not go about on it. No lion will be there, nor any ravenous beast; they will not be found there. But only the redeemed will walk there, and those the LORD has rescued will return. They will enter Zion with singing; everlasting joy will crown their heads. Gladness and joy will overtake them, and sorrow and sighing will flee away (Isa. 35:1–10 NIV).

God is a God of restoration, and He planned your restoration. He has gone before you, and He is waiting for you to hold out your hand so He can walk with you to new life. I know it may not seem possible at this point, so it is my hope that you will begin to see a glimmer of light in the darkness. I have walked this journey, and it does get brighter. Jesus is with you every step of this journey. He promises to never leave or forsake you. He is an ever-present help in time of need. Will you take His hand and walk with Him in this desert place?

This book began as a series of Holy Spirit-inspired messages given to me while serving as a minister of pastoral care. These messages have been shared in ministry with those who were broken, abused, and hurting. The Lord used my journey as a springboard to help others. We are all connected, and I do also believe that a part of God's bigger plan is to use our suffering to help others so God might be glorified. This journey is objective and can apply to anyone who has experienced hurt.

I am here to testify that what the enemy came to destroy or what has been taken or lost, Jesus came to give back. As stated earlier, "The thief comes only to steal and kill and destroy; I have come that they may have life, and have it to the full. 'I am the good shepherd. The good shepherd lays down his life for the sheep'" (John 10:10–11). I pray that the Savior will touch you as you read this book and you will realize how much God loves you.

As you journey through these messages, I will take you to the cross and release you to Jesus, who promises to never leave or forsake you. He will walk with you through your suffering, and my prayer is that you will take His hand and walk with Him, having Him lead you each day and each step of your pain and your life. As you take His hand, He promises to never leave or forsake you, a very present help in time of need. Remember, this is a process and a personal relationship with Jesus, who is alive today.

Sunday afternoons are a special time on the beaches of Charleston, SC for both tourists and locals. You are likely to find people enjoying the day or sharing the fresh air with their dogs. One Sunday afternoon, our family came across an injured butterfly near the surf. It seemed the butterfly was gasping its last breath. We carried it and placed it in an area away from the wind. As it lay there, we began releasing words of encouragement to it, speaking words of life and strength, as if it were a person. As we did, it was as if the little butterfly heard our words. It began flapping its wings, and soon it took off in flight.

You know, sometimes life can knock the wind out of our sails. Words are powerful, and it is my sincere hope that, as you read the words of this journey, you will gain the same strength and hope in Jesus, just as that little butterfly did.

The power of the cross transforms lives. Jesus came to redeem and to restore; to give back all that has been taken in life's journey. Because of Jesus' shed blood and work on the cross, we can find healing. Jesus is alive today and He is our only source of hope. God's unfailing love restores and redeems our lives. Isaiah prophesied Jesus's ministry years before He was born. God foretold His plan of redemption. There had to be shed blood for forgiveness of sin; there had to be a wounding before there could be a healing. And also, this amazing grace gives us strength for the journey. The cross was God's rescue plan for us. When Jesus ascended to heaven, He also left us a powerful helper, the Holy Spirit. God knew your name before the foundation of the earth, and He planned your rescue, to give not only salvation but healing from all brokenness.

God promises to never leave you or forsake you. God is faithful to us even when we mess up. God loves us even in our rebellion and, through the prophet Isaiah, prophesied the great deliverer, Jesus Christ, the one who would redeem us. God sent Jesus to die on the cross to bring us to relationship with Jesus and to bring restoration and healing to us, to take what the enemy comes to do and to turn our ashes into something beautiful.

The power of the blood of Jesus heals our wounds. We all have wounds that need healing. Some may be fresh; others may be from decades ago that have never been released and healed. So as you journey in the process, you may find the Holy Spirit bringing up some wounds from years ago that Jesus wants to heal. He did that for me. Also, as we journey, I will be using the following scripture at different parts of the book as we reflect on this beautiful exchange.

> The Spirit of the Sovereign LORD is on me, because the LORD has anointed me to proclaim good news to the poor. He has sent me to bind up the brokenhearted, to proclaim freedom for the captives and release from darkness for the prisoners, to proclaim the year of the LORD's favor and the day of vengeance of our God, to comfort all who mourn, and provide for those who grieve in Zion—to bestow on them a crown of beauty instead of ashes, the oil of joy instead of mourning, and a garment of praise instead of a spirit of despair. They will be called oaks of righteousness, a planting of the LORD for the display of his splendor. They will rebuild the ancient ruins and restore the places long devastated; they will renew the ruined cities that have been devastated for generations. Strangers will shepherd your flocks; foreigners will work your fields and vineyards. And you will be called priests of the LORD, you will be named ministers of our God. You will feed on the wealth of nations, and in their riches you will boast. Instead of your shame you will receive a double portion, and instead of disgrace you will rejoice in your

inheritance. And so you will inherit a double portion in your land, and everlasting joy will be yours. "For I, the LORD, love justice; I hate robbery and wrongdoing. In my faithfulness I will reward my people and make an everlasting covenant with them. Their descendants will be known among the nations and their offspring among the peoples. All who see them will acknowledge that they are a people the LORD has blessed." I delight greatly in the LORD; my soul rejoices in my God. For he has clothed me with garments of salvation and arrayed me in a robe of his righteousness, as a bridegroom adorns his head like a priest, and as a bride adorns herself with her jewels. For as the soil makes the sprout come up and a garden causes seeds to grow, so the Sovereign LORD will make righteousness and praise spring up before all nations (Isa. 61:1–11).

Isaiah 61 reflects perfectly the prophecy of Jesus Christ and His earthly ministry. When Jesus stood in the town of Nazareth in the synagogue, He opened the scrolls and read part of this very scripture written by Isaiah many years before His birth.

Jesus returned to Galilee in the power of the Spirit, and news about Him spread through the whole countryside. He was teaching in their synagogues, and everyone praised Him. He went to Nazareth, where He had been brought up, and on the Sabbath day, he went into the synagogue, as was his custom. He stood up to read, and the scroll of the prophet Isaiah was handed to Him. Unrolling it, He found the place where it is written,

"The Spirit of the Lord is on me, because he has anointed me to proclaim good news to the poor. He has sent me to proclaim freedom for the prisoners and recovery of sight for the blind, to set the oppressed free, to proclaim the year of the Lord's favor." Then he rolled up the scroll, gave it back to the attendant and sat down. The

eyes of everyone in the synagogue were fastened on him.
He began by saying to them, "Today this scripture is
fulfilled in your hearing" (Luke 4:14–21).

Not only was Isaiah 61 real during Jesus's earthly ministry, I am
here to personally proclaim that Jesus is alive today. We worship a risen
Savior who promises to never leave or forsake us. God's plan of salvation
in sending His only Son Jesus to the earth was also intended to offer the
great exchanges written in Isaiah 61. Jesus is still performing miracles
today, saving and healing those who cry out to Him. He is in the
business of freeing the captive. God still woos us to a place of freedom.

We will be discussing lies and truth during this journey. Lies are
anything that is counter to what God says about us. Lies are deceptions
from the enemy. Truth is what God says about us, that is, what His
Word says about us. Much of the bondage in our lives is due to lies that
we have accepted as truth from the enemy. Oftentimes these lies take
root at the point of trauma, abuse, and hurt.

**Jesus came to heal your broken heart, to free you from all captivity,
to comfort you when you mourn, to bestow on you a crown of
beauty for ashes, and to turn your despair into joy and praise.**

Praise God! "I have told you these things, so that in me you may
have peace. In this world you will have trouble. But take heart! I have
overcome the world" (John 16:33). Because of Jesus's shed blood on the
cross, we can be free, healed, and delivered.

I wrote this book because I have seen this in my own life and I want
to share this truth with others like you. God knew your name before
the creation, and He made a plan to send His only Son, Jesus, to be the
perfect sacrifice for the sins of mankind. Our sins nailed him on the
cross; our sins were the thorns in His head. Because God knew blood
had to be shed for the forgiveness of sin, this wounding brings a healing.

Jesus died, and He was resurrected. He is alive today. He died to
restore you. At the moment we ask Jesus to come into our hearts, we
receive salvation. In addition, we are sealed with the Holy Spirit. This

means that the Holy Spirit resides within us. The Holy Spirit is our helper, and two ways He does this are to guide us and to reveal truth to us. As we walk in relationship with Jesus and we open our hearts and share our painful wounds, opening our wounds to the healing light of Jesus, we receive healing. Christ sets us free by the power of His blood. "For to us a child is born, to us a son is given, and the government will be on his shoulders. And he will be called Wonderful Counselor, Mighty God, Everlasting Father, Prince of Peace" (Isa. 9:6).

"But the Advocate, the Holy Spirit, whom the Father will send in my name, will teach you all things and will remind you of everything I have said to you" (John 14:26). So where is God when we suffer? He is right here with us, calling us to surrender all of it to Him.

When devastation hits, we look around, and everything seems destroyed, like a desert without hope. Life as we knew it seems shattered; our dreams are broken. As we sit in the shock and ashes of our reality, Jesus weeps with us. Because of Jesus, we have hope, and as He holds out His hand to pick us up from these ashes, we stand up and take one step at a time of this journey toward new life. One day, full restoration will happen, and the desert will be as Isaiah 35 describes. However, because of the power of Jesus's blood that was shed on the cross, today we can have new life.

Mankind despised and rejected Jesus. He was a man of suffering and familiar with pain. Like one from whom people hide their faces, He was despised, and we held Him in low esteem. Surely He took up our pain and bore our suffering, yet we considered Him punished by God, stricken by Him, and afflicted. But He was pierced for our transgressions, and He was crushed for our iniquities. The punishment that brought us peace was on Him, and by His wounds, we are healed. We all, like sheep, have gone astray. Each of us has turned to our own way, and the LORD has laid on him the iniquity of us all (Isa. 53:3–6).

He carried our sickness and our pains, and He bore our sin. He was a man of pain, our sorrow, and our pain. Jesus died on the cross, and when He ascended into heaven, He left us the gift of the Holy Spirit, our helper. God's great grace gives us salvation as well as strength for the journey. Jesus carried our sin. Our sin nailed Him to the cross, and because of the powerful work of the cross, Jesus has overcome sin and death. Because of His sacrifice, we can surrender our lives, our hearts, our pain, and our suffering to Him. God wants to heal your heart. He sent his only Son to die for you. By His wounds, we are healed. Because of Jesus's blood that was shed on the cross, we can experience healing and restoration, God's divine plan from the start.

Many people wonder where God is when they suffer. Does He care about me? God loved us so much that He sent His Son. His priority was to offer the great exchanges of Isaiah 61 and the overcoming of sin. He knew you before time. Jesus said, "in this world, you will have trouble. But take heart. I have overcome the world" (John 16:33). Jesus was a suffering servant. He was not just a man, but God Himself who came to earth despised and rejected. Where is God when you suffer? He is with you, calling you to surrender and allow Him to carry the suffering so He can give you the grace you need and the healing you so desperately need.

As humans, when we suffer, we begin to feel that God has left us. We may think that God is holding out on us and could have stopped this in some way. So why didn't He? We feel forsaken. Believe me. I understand. Whatever you are experiencing, Jesus endured it first. This means we have Jesus, who understands what we go through. You cannot experience any pain that Christ does not understand. Will you take Jesus's hand and walk with Him, allowing Him to take the burden from you?

Our sins were the thorns in Christ's head, the nails in his hands and feet, and the spear in his side. He was delivered to death for our offenses. Jesus died the worst possible means of dying, on a Roman cross so that, because of His blood, by His wounds we are healed.

"But he was pierced for our transgressions, he was crushed for our iniquities; the punishment that brought us peace was on him, and by his wounds we are healed" (Isa. 53:5). "And we know that in all things God works for the good of those who love him, who have been called according to his purpose" (Rom. 8:28).

God does this very thing with our lives. Sometimes hurts and pain in our lives can serve as a catalyst to healing. The suffering in my life was the very thing that God used to heal me. Though you may be in the middle of a traumatic situation, feeling hopeless, I am here to tell you that the very thing that has left you feeling broken can be the very thing that God uses to heal, restore, and redeem you.

I believe these three words can change your life: I surrender all.

God used a devotion that I turned to on a morning when I woke, feeling broken after a week of bringing past hurt from my childhood before the Lord. This came about because I had noticed I was overreacting to a particular situation in my life. When I prayed about why I was doing this, the Holy Spirit revealed a childhood wound to me. Can I be real here? I felt emotionally raw.

How many of you have ever felt that way? God is so faithful. He knew I needed encouragement that morning. On that day, God confirmed that nothing brought before the throne and shared with Him is ever wasted. He was going to redeem the broken pieces of my past. I share this because, during this journey, I will begin to share with you the things I have learned about how the Holy Spirit is our helper in the healing process.

I challenge you to begin asking the Holy Spirit to show you areas that you need to surrender and bring to Jesus for healing. Remember that this is a process, a journey. This is the beginning of taking the broken pieces of our lives and allowing God to make something beautiful out of the ashes. Will you begin to allow the Holy Spirit to reveal areas of your life that you need to surrender? It might be bitterness, deep hurt, or betrayal. Is your heart broken? Does fear and worry grip you? Are you in deep hurt and pain? Are you traumatized, abused, disappointed, angry, and unable to forgive? We will learn how to take these matters before the Lord for healing. Begin to allow God to remove these burdens from your shoulders and allow God to be God. God has this and He has you.

Something about a journey ignites hope. As you start your path, realizing this is a journey, begin to imagine the hope that awaits you. Are you beginning to see a few sparkles of joy and hope on the route as we approach the first step onto this journey to new life?

Jesus is reaching out for your hand. Are you ready to surrender your life and pain to Him? Are you ready to trade your sorrow? If you are, I promise you that Jesus is alive today and in the business of restoration and healing. So grab your journal and reach out your hand.

> You answer us with awesome and righteous deeds, God our Savior, the hope of all the ends of the earth and of the farthest seas, who formed the mountains by your power, having armed yourself with strength, who stilled the roaring of the seas, the roaring of their waves, and the turmoil of the nations. The whole earth is filled with awe at your wonders; where morning dawns, where evening fades, you call forth songs of joy" (Ps. 65:5–8).

CHAPTER 2

Nothing Is Impossible with God

It was the darkest day in human history. Jesus had been crucified, and all seemed hopeless. The Savior and Deliverer, the Redeemer of Israel, had been brutally executed. I wonder: Do you feel hopeless as you sit in the darkness of your situation?

After Jesus was buried, Mary Magdalene and the other Mary went to look at Jesus's tomb. As they approached the tomb, an earthquake happened, and the stone that had been placed at the entrance to the tomb rolled off. Afterward an angel appeared and sat on the stone. The angel told the women not to be afraid.

What is it about loss, grief, and seemingly hopeless situations that cause us to fear? One of most prevalent fears out there is a fear of losing control. Part of the reason I believe this is so is because, as we come face-to-face with the fact that we do not control life or in the way we'd like to think we do, it scares us. God is the only one in control. And one of the biggest fears we have when something horrible happens is how we will ever survive this new reality. So we may work in our own strength to control and get things back to normal.

It was a beautiful afternoon, and I headed out to run. As I approached the location, I had a sense of fear. I circled around the area, not sure what was happening. Why was I feeling fear? So I parked my car. Okay, I was going. My fear would not go away. What was happening? So I drove away and started to go home. I then thought, *What am I doing? This makes no sense.*

Finally I made a choice. I was going to run and run afraid if I had to do so. As I went out to run, hundreds of people were enjoying the day. There was such an atmosphere of joy all around that day, even among the many dogs who were running and jumping. As I ran, I still had that little edge of fear on me. Have you ever heard of the word described with the first letters of FEAR, "False evidence appearing real"? Well, that was happening.

But God was teaching me a few things about fear that afternoon. The first was about choice. I had to make a choice to believe I was safe to step out and run. I had to know that God had me. As I ran, I began to reflect on God's character. The joy was still there, even in my fear. As I ran, I recalled that sometimes we have to come face-to-face with our fears when we step out. And occasionally we have to run afraid. And when we do, we have no choice but to keep going.

I began to recognize that day I was very focused on the fearful and negative things. And when we do just that, then they seem huge. However, when we concentrate on God and His character, then God becomes more powerful than our circumstance. I believe God was reminding me of something that day. I needed to remind myself of just how big of a God I serve. He is sovereign, all-powerful, omniscient, and omnipotent. He is ruler and master of the universe. When I do this, hope fills me. When I realize what God can do in one second to change everything, I have hope even in a fearful circumstance.

The God of the universe is always with us. We usually have the most fear when we are in what appears to be a hopeless situation. But we must remember that nothing is impossible with God, He who did not spare even His own Son for our salvation. He is the God of hope, the blessed hope. He is our joy and our hope.

As I drove home that day after my run, I stopped at a stoplight while making a left turn. By chance, I glanced over and noticed a young man in the car beside me. As I did, he just looked very lost and hopeless, so I turned the radio up loud so he might hear a song of hope. I began thinking of Ezekiel 37, the dead bones to life prophecy. Who does that? Right at a stoplight?

I chuckled and began to remember my run that afternoon. One of the most noticeable things was the landscape of the area. Perhaps because it was a fall day, a time where everything looks to die in preparation for the winter, it appeared to have an air of fear from seemingly hopeless dead places. You know, when things around us appear hopeless, isn't that when we become fearful? To me, the fear today was a reminder of this reality and the importance of facing that fright.

But guess what? When everything everywhere seems dead, God is about to do something. He is about to restore all of the dead, dry bones. The lost will be found. The unfulfilled promises of redemption and restoration are about to happen. Spring is coming when everything appearing dead will come to life. God is a God of hope, healing, and restoration. Nothing is impossible with God!

It is always darkest before dawn. Have you ever heard that expression? It is true in our lives also. In this world, Jesus said, "I have told you these things, so that in me you may have peace. In this world you will have trouble. But take heart! I have overcome the world" (John 16:33). All of the horrible hurts and suffering in our lives are not the end all to be all. Because of Jesus, we have hope! Because He was crucified, we have the hope of restoration and that all of the dead bones of our lives and the lives of others will come to life. And when they do, we will have joy unspeakable!

As I continue, I will be sharing a Holy Spirit-inspired message that was given to me. My prayer is that it will provide encouragement and hope to you as you face your fear. Psalm 27 says,

> The LORD is my light and my salvation—whom shall I fear? The LORD is the stronghold of my life—of whom shall I be afraid? When the wicked advance against me to devour me, it is my enemies and my foes who will stumble and fall. Though an army besiege me, my heart will not fear; though war break out against me, even then I will be confident. One thing I ask from the LORD, this only do I seek: that I may dwell in the house of the LORD all the days of my life, to gaze on the beauty of the LORD and to seek him in his temple. For in the

day of trouble he will keep me safe in his dwelling; he will hide me in the shelter of his sacred tent and set me high upon a rock. Then my head will be exalted above the enemies who surround me; at his sacred tent I will sacrifice with shouts of joy; I will sing and make music to the LORD. Hear my voice when I call, LORD; be merciful to me and answer me. My heart says of you, "Seek his face!" Your face, LORD, I will seek. Do not hide your face from me, do not turn your servant away in anger; you have been my helper. Do not reject me or forsake me, God my Savior. Though my father and mother forsake me, the LORD will receive me. Teach me your way, LORD; lead me in a straight path because of my oppressors. Do not turn me over to the desire of my foes, for false witnesses rise up against me, spouting malicious accusations. I remain confident of this: I will see the goodness of the LORD in the land of the living. Wait for the LORD; be strong and take heart and wait for the LORD.

This scripture was written against a backdrop of trouble, danger, and great fear. David, the author, is probably responding to one of many times of great trouble and fear. Are you in a fearful situation right now? If so, I pray that this message will give you courage as you continue on your journey. This is one of the messages of hope that was Holy Spirit-inspired. So read it as you like. One of my favorite is to read it like you are at a pep rally. Remember those in high school. Oh my, maybe not? Anyhow at a pep rally, you have the coach giving a pep talk, getting everyone excited about the team. Is this where we are right now as you read this? Do we need an old-fashioned pep talk? If so, give me a H. Give me an O. Give me a P. Give me an E. What does it spell? Hope! Nothing is impossible with God.

In the midst of his distress, David begins with an affirmation of faith and confidence in God. How did he face his fear with such confidence? Faith. He chose to believe God. That God was his light, the one who guided him. He was His salvation, the one to deliver him. And He was his stronghold, the one to protect him.

And so an event happens, perhaps a crisis, illness, accident, job loss, relationship issue, trauma, or betrayal; something that rocks our world. It often times hits us unexpectedly, and we find ourselves gripped with fear. We can feel paralyzed with no way out and no hope for change. Frequently things can look impossible, which only drives our emotion of fear. Oftentimes we go into ourselves. We isolate ourselves. We begin to strive to fix things, figure out the solution, restore it, and somehow get things back the way they were. The last thing on our mind is to take the matter to God and leave it with Him. After all, we have this thing figured out. We know we will have it resolved with a little time. This thing consumes us. At these times, we find ourselves staring in the face of fear.

What is fear? Webster's Dictionary 1913 defines fear as "to be in apprehension of evil; to be afraid; to feel anxiety on account of some expected evil." Being afraid is not wrong in itself. As people living in a fallen world, we should be afraid at times. The problem is when fear forgets God. In the above psalm, David took his fear to God. He was aware of his fear of people, but he took the matter before God. David is an inspiration to us in our times of fear as we meditate on the psalms with faith and follow David's example.

Jesus looked at them and said, "With man this is impossible, but with God all things are possible" (Matt. 19:26). We see the situation as big or impossible because we see only one solution, the logical way, but there is an alternative, faith. God can do impossible things.

David met his fears head-on. He said "I remain confident of this: I will see the goodness of the LORD in the land of the living" (Psalm 27:13). How did he do it? Faith. He chose to believe in God. That God is his light, the one to guide him. That God is his salvation, the one to deliver him. That God was his stronghold, the one to protect him. David reasoned that, if God were his light, salvation, and stronghold, then whom should he fear in comparison to a powerful God?

David had faith and realized nothing was impossible with God. He surrendered his situation to God, stopped trying to resolve it himself, and waited on God to do it. He prayed about it, surrendered the matter, left it there, and believed God would do it. When we face obstacles, one of the reasons it looks bleak is we only see one option, the most logical. But there is an alternative, faith.

I am here to testify that this is the time to put away those running shoes and to go to our knees and talk to God about all of it. Jesus said, "I have told you these things, so that in me you may have peace. In this world you will have trouble. But take heart! I have overcome the world" (John 16.33). And Psalm 55:22 says, "Cast your cares on the LORD and he will sustain you; he will never let the righteous be shaken."

In these times, which can linger on for a long time, these are the times of refining and building our faith. There are times when we have to face our fears. God promises in the Bible, "Be strong and courageous. Do not be afraid or terrified because of them, for the LORD your God goes with you; he will never leave you nor forsake you" (Deut. 31:6). God will walk with you through your suffering and the crippling fear. This week I'm asking you to walk with me, as I do the same in my life, through a fear in your life. Pray about it. Take it to the Lord. If you need to, journal it. And then surrender it to God. Come face-to-face with your fear, and cast your cares upon the Lord. God is mighty to save. This is how faith is built. It is in the trenches when we depend on a mighty God.

Have you ever had this thing that you are holding onto while at the same time you are in relationship with Jesus? However, you have no eye contact with the Lord when you pray because you are secretly angry at God for allowing this thing to happen? Can we be real here? How can a loving God allow this to happen? I'm talking about getting real with God and talking about all of the things you are struggling with and can't figure out. Get mad. God is big, and He can handle that. I'm here to testify that our purpose in life is not to feel all warm and fuzzy. It is to glorify God. Other people are watching us, and if we find strength in the Lord during our time of great need, others will be drawn to the cross and our hope.

And what is our hope? "So we fix our eyes not on what is seen, but on what is unseen, since what is seen is temporary, but what is unseen is eternal" (2 Cor. 4:18). When we experience difficult times, Jesus is repeatedly telling us to focus on the indescribable, eternal glory more than we concentrate on the temporary sufferings. This is by no means easy, and it is not meant to be. In my journey, I have found that surrendering the pain and situation to God is the solution. When I did do this, I received a sequin of hope called grace. And once grace showed up, I finally had rest and peace, which I had not had for many years.

And now let's go back to our scripture. What were the fearful circumstances that David was facing? Certain people were against him and after him. They were out to take away his land, his kingdom, and his life. Armies were threatening him, and war was on the horizon. Wow! Could anything else possibly go wrong? Have you ever felt this way? Do you feel this way now? What if that fear is of a person? First, let me ask. Is any person greater than God? Who is God? What are His characteristics? During these times, we need God's Word to remind us just who we worship.

Saul, David's great enemy, chased David for years in a pursuit to kill him. Why? Let's be honest. Saul was jealous. Saul was Israel's first king for forty-two years. God removed his crown because he was not obedient. Nor did he trust God. God had told him to destroy the Amalekites and all of their possessions, and he did not do it. The Lord withdrew his favor and had the prophet Samuel anoint David as king. Later David killed Goliath. As the Jewish women were dancing in a victory parade, they sang, "Saul has slain his thousands, and David his tens of thousands" (1 Sam. 18:7). After which, Saul went into a rage and became jealous of David, and he vowed to kill him.

Each time that we find ourselves captive to fear, we have forgotten God's character. I challenge you this week to remember God's character, write it down on paper, and read it daily until you believe it. Here is my list to help you with yours. God is sovereign, which means He is in control of everything. God is all-powerful, the only true God. He is the Alpha and the Omega, Lord, protector, faithful, and Savior. He is omniscient, which means He knows everything. He is the Great I Am, ruler, and master of the world. God is our rock and refuge, a very present help in times of trouble. Wow! That's some résumé, and this is just the tip of the iceberg. Facing our fears means taking God's Word and reading it to remind us of His character.

Another important thing to do with our fear is to ask for wisdom when we are up against a fearful challenge. David knew the key to wisdom in his fearful situation was to seek an answer from the Lord.

> When David learned that Saul was plotting against him, he said to Abiathar the priest, "Bring the ephod." David said, "LORD, God of Israel, your servant has heard definitely that Saul plans to come to Keilah and destroy the town on account of me. Will the citizens of Keilah surrender me to him? Will Saul come down, as your servant has heard? LORD, God of Israel, tell your servant." And the LORD said, "He will." Again David asked, "Will the citizens of Keilah surrender me and my men to Saul?" And the LORD said, "They will." So David and his men, about six hundred in number, left Keilah and kept moving from place to place. When Saul was told that David had escaped from Keilah, he did not go there. David stayed in the wilderness strongholds and in the hills of the Desert of Ziph. Day after day Saul searched for him, but God did not give David into his hands" (1 Sam. 23:9–14).

In this scripture, David reveals another truth. When faced with fear, we need to pray for guidance of what to do and where to go for safety so we can praise. God tells David what to do. During these times, it is important to seek God's help and wisdom. God promises wisdom.

Fear is normal when there is danger. God gave us fear to protect us and to get us away from danger. God is aware of you. He loves you. He sees you and your individual situations. And above all, remember that it is not your fault when someone hurts you.

Just for a moment, I'd like to contrast two circumstances where one individual in the Bible did not face his fears head-on but trusted in himself and his own strategy. And the other did face his fear head-on and trusted God. Am I speaking to someone here? Abraham and David are my two examples of people in the Bible who feared man at some points but handled it in very different ways.

> As he was about to enter Egypt, he said to his wife Sarai, "I know what a beautiful woman you are. When the Egyptians see you, they will say, 'This is his wife.' Then they will kill me but will let you live. Say you are my sister, so that I will be treated well for your sake and my life will be spared because of you" (Gen. 12:11–13).

Rather than trusting God, Abraham had faith in his own self-protective schemes. Has anyone here ever done that? Abraham feared man more than God. He was afraid he would be killed, so he devised this scheme. Now let's contrast this to David in his situation. David was afraid, but he did not fear people over God, as Abraham did in the particular situation. He did fear, but he took it to the Lord.

David asked, "When I am afraid, I put my trust in you. In God, whose word I praise—in God I trust and am not afraid. What can mere mortals do to me?" (Ps. 56:3–4). God was David's rock and fortress.

What was the difference between these two men? Both were in real life threatening danger, and both had rational, natural fear. One chose to trust in God and the other chose not to but chose to trust in himself. During these moments of fear, it is a choice to trust God or not. Finally I'd like to add that these two men were individuals of great faith, so don't beat yourself up if you struggle. God is mighty to save!

In Psalm 27, David made a choice in the midst of his distress. David begins the psalm with an affirmation of his faith and confidence in God, not with a request of God. How did he face this fear with such confidence? Faith.

In the face of threatening people and times, David wants and pursues one thing over all. "One thing I ask from the LORD, this only do I seek: that I may dwell in the house of the LORD all the days of my life, to gaze on the beauty of the LORD and to seek him in his temple" (Ps. 27:4).

What one thing would you ask of God in your situation? Would your request and desire be the same as David? Would you long to be in God's presence and in unbroken fellowship with Him? Would you long to worship and gaze upon God's beauty? Why would this be his desire? Why is it important that this also be ours? David chose faith again. He wanted to stay close to God because he knew that, when he was in trouble, God would be his safe haven and help.

Here I emphasize that prayer is the prescription for fear. "Do not be anxious about anything, but in every situation, by prayer and petition, with thanksgiving, present your requests to God. And the peace of God, which transcends all understanding, will guard your hearts and your minds in Christ Jesus" (Phil. 4:6–7). As we release our fears and our anxiety to God, we experience peace.

We are all born with a void that only a relationship with God can fill. We are born with a nature that knows that there is something out there much bigger than we are. As humans, no matter how many riches we acquire, we will always desire more. When we do not allow God to fill this void, we will seek man-made idols to fill this void. Some examples are relationships, careers, houses, cars, money, fame, success, status, and clothes, and the list goes on and on. When we do this, we create a false sense of security in these idols, and if anything threatens to take them away, we experience great fear.

We've spoken of the big fears, but let's talk about the smaller day-to-day fears. When we think of idolatry, we often think of worshipping a graven image. But I'm here to tell you that anything that is placed higher than God in our lives is an idol. In the Bible, there are examples of the people bowing down to the work of their hands and what their fingers made. How do we do this? When we allow our jobs and careers to become our source of value, security, comfort and prestige. Many idols are false strategies of comfort and security. These will never fulfil our lives. I know this by experience. I was very career-driven, and I know how temporal its success can be and how it does not compare to placing Jesus at the center of my life.

"The lord is near to those who call on Him, who call on Him in truth" (Ps. 145:18). When we come before God, say that we have been believing the lie that our idol is more important to us than He is, and acknowledge it is not working, this brings freedom. I remember the day I begged God to open the door so I would get the job of my dreams, a position I thought would rock my world. I was afraid that, if I did not get this job, I would be less important as a person. I was receiving my value as a person from my career.

I know what fear looks like. I've feared losing my career and not using my talent to bless other people. I've feared anything hurting my children. I've feared starting out fresh. You name it. I've feared it. But each time I took my fear to the Lord and claimed His promises, I received peace, strength, and grace in my time of need. The opposite of fear is faith. We must choose to believe and trust in God's character. This is a choice. God is always faithful.

Psalm 27 revolves around one question: Whom will I fear, God or people? When David was afraid, he remembered that people could have great power compared to him, but they had no power compared to God. The better we know God, the more we will trust Him. The more we trust Him, the more we will sense His peace when the difficult winds come. When we stay connected with God through prayer, we will have a continual supply of strength to walk victoriously. "You will keep in perfect peace those whose minds are steadfast, because they trust in you" (Isa. 26:3).

Next, David brings up the subject of praise. When I was in the youth choir at my church, I would sometimes lip-sync the songs because I did not think I had a nice voice. Okay, now am I the only one? The praise David is speaking of is singing songs from the heart to God, not worrying what others might think. David is sure that God will give him something to cheer about, to sing about, even in circumstances that might otherwise make him a nervous wreck. "Then my head will be exulted above the enemies who surround me; at his sacred tent I will sacrifice with shouts of joy; I will sing and make music to the Lord" (Psalm 27:6).

And finally in 2 Samuel 22, David sang a song of praise to God who had just delivered him from his enemies. He always gave the glory to God. Praise is powerful. When we praise, the enemy must flee. Take time to praise God for times of deliverance in your life and your blessings. Our praise is a weapon. When we praise, worship, and meditate on God's Word, it takes our mind off our fears and onto a powerful God.

We must pray in the difficult times of life and praise God for deliverance and salvation. This praise is an act of trust and faith. And how do we build our faith to make it stronger? We stay in communication with God, not just when things aren't going well. It is a personal relationship. In addition, we can read our Bible, keep scriptures handy that have deep meaning to us, entrust our lives to the Lord, and remember times of victory that can be recalled when in a difficult time. These are all faith builders.

Let's go back to our scripture. Suddenly everything is different. David moves from a statement of confidence in God to an anxious prayer. Why? Now he is praying for God's mercy. David realizes that his good works are nothing but filthy rags and there is no merit in him. David has been asking and expecting (having faith) that God will guide, save, and protect him, but not on the basis of his own moral behavior that he knows he falls short of. No, his hope lies in God's mercy, which gives him hope that God might be willing to keep him safe in the day of trouble in spite of his sin.

The worst thing that could happen is for God to hide His face. David recognizes that, but for the grace and mercy of God, he has no hope. But he trusts and believes that God is willing to listen to him anyway, which is his great hope. How often do we look at our own behavior and think God may do that for that person, but not me? I've messed up too much. It's not true. We all fall short of the glory of God. During these times, we need to remember David. Will you take the time to call on God's mercy? Will you ask God for help? He is already right here, waiting for your call.

David concludes with an affirmation of his confidence in God in depressing and fearful circumstances. He expresses faith and confidence that God will work all things for good and knows that his best days are ahead. So much so that he tells us to have the same confidence in our fearful times, when it is difficult to see the good and when evil seems to win. He tells us to wait for the Lord. Be patient. Believe that your best days are ahead and to be confident that you will see the goodness of the Lord in your situation. And so faith is the key to victory over our fears in difficult, often dangerous, and trying times. "I remain confident of this: I will see the goodness of the LORD in the land of the living" (Ps. 27:13).

As I was preparing this message, a particular fear in my life came to mind. During this time, I finally took the time to pray and turn to God, crying out for help. For you see, I had been struggling with a lot of fear and worry. What I realized was that the Lord was allowing me to experience situations that made me afraid to build my spiritual muscles. Much like an athlete lifts weights to build muscle, we must take action in our times of fear. What I learned is that when I stepped out and faced the fear, I experienced peace. These were my greatest growth opportunities.

God is mighty to save. With one touch from Him, everything can change. God is the God of the impossible. Nothing is impossible with God. As I reflect on this truth, I get it. Will you?

CHAPTER 3

Garment of Praise for a Spirit of Despair

Have you ever been in despair over a loss? I'm talking about the deep pit of hopelessness, where you logically cannot see how this could ever be used for good. The pain is so deep and far-reaching that you wonder, "How can this ever bring anything but hopelessness?" I am challenging you today to hold on. There is hope.

I have learned that very often my greatest times of deliverance have been when I took the time to cry out to the Lord for help. It does not matter whether you are crying out for the first time ever or have been in a relationship with the Lord for years. You see, in my situation, I had been in a relationship with God, but I was angry, not looking directly at God. I was angry because I was hurt. One particular day, I took all of my feelings to the Lord. I was open and honest about what I was feeling and thinking. To be completely honest, I was in despair without hope.

As you know, these messages are Holy Spirit-inspired messages. I decided to place this message closer to the beginning of the journey and not later as it was originally because I believe that despair overrides a lot of our emotions when we have experienced loss. And it is important to recognize that these times can lead to questioning everything, even God. God promises "the oil of joy instead of mourning, and a garment of praise for a spirit of despair" (Isa. 61:3). This hope is real.

In these times of great despair, my prayer is for you to find even a small glitter of joy in the darkness. Please do not beat yourself up if it takes you a while, like it did me. God wants to hear from you, so pray and journal. No matter what or how you feel, Jesus loves you. He is with you every second in every detail. Jesus cries with you. Let Him hold you and have this. He died for this.

God shared this fact that He is indeed with me as I shared my heartache, pain, and anger, all of it. He is with you also. Even when you don't feel like this is true, it still is. No matter how you feel, you must choose to trust in God and who He is, and sometimes that might be all you have to hold onto. I promise you that, whatever your journey looks like, you will get to new life. I know it because I did. It is a journey, a process.

One of the reasons I decided to share this journey with you is to impart the hope that I found on my journey. There is life on the other side of this pain. And there is also healing and restoration. So please hang onto that sparkle of glitter, the joy, the hope. It is there. Right now, you may not see it, and that's okay. Just cry and feel the pain. Journal it, and release it to Jesus. If you pick it right back up the next day, that's okay. You will finally and fully release it one day at just the right time.

Just because we don't believe or doubt something, it doesn't mean it is less true. And when tragedy and heartache strikes, disbelief and anger also arrive on the scene.

Sometimes the only thing we have to hold onto is glimmers of light that we may catch as we stumble through the moment. The Bible says, "We are blessed when we mourn, because we will be comforted. Blessed are those who mourn, for they will be comforted" (Matt 5:4). This comfort comes from Immanuel. God is with us. He promises to comfort us.

Have you ever looked up at the stars at night or sat on a crisp, dark winter night and enjoyed the beautiful lights on your Christmas tree? Have you ever noticed the beauty of candlelight or walked along the beach at night and enjoyed the reflection of the moon off the water? What is it about light, particularly light that contrasts the darkness surrounding us at the time? What is it about light that reaches into our darkness with glimmers of hope and beauty? Think about that for a moment.

What is it about light that lifts our spirits? For purposes of this message, I define light as hope or lifting up of our Spirit. For me personally, the Lord used a time of darkness and strengthened my faith and taught me to hope, to look for the light. This burden deeply tested my faith. God laid on my heart on one winter day this particular truth, and only three months later did I find myself in the morning singing praises to God. On this one particular morning, I surprised myself that, after waking up and thanking God for little things, I began to sing. That was my epiphany. It was something so simple, yet I had overlooked the light because I was so overwhelmed by the darkness that my complete focus had become the darkness.

Have you ever found yourself here? Then all of sudden out of nowhere, I found myself singing songs of praise, and these were coming from my heart. I share this because I want you to know that God understands how difficult it is to put on a "garment of praise instead of a spirit of despair" (Isaiah 61:3). It is not easy, but I believe it is possible. And I believe that light provides the glimmer of hope that makes it possible for this praise. But you ask, "What is this light of which you speak?" I promise that you will see it. Hope never fades, even in the darkness.

"And provide for those who grieve in Zion—to bestow on them a crown of beauty instead of ashes, the oil of joy instead of mourning, and a garment of praise instead of a spirit of despair. They will be called oaks of righteousness, a planting of the LORD for the display of his splendor" (Isa. 61:3).

How many of you today are feeling hopeless? For me, this message is one of the more difficult ones to deliver because, in order to impart the missive, I've had to face a seemingly hopeless situation. And how can I ask you to praise God in the midst of your hopeless situation? Could you offer God praise when you have lost your loved one? When you have lost your home, your job or your spouse? Could God be asking us to be different despite the circumstances? How do we praise God in those times when we find ourselves in complete despair?

In a message filled with contrasts of light and darkness, I'd like to make five points:

- Darkness can build our faith, leading to praising Him despite the circumstance.

- Often we won't search for the light unless it gets dark.
- Darkness can lead to hope and healing.
- A healing can come from a wounding.
- God's grace strengthens us for the journey.

"When Jesus spoke again to the people, he said, 'I am the light of the world. Whoever follows me will never walk in darkness, but will have the light of life'" (John 8:12). Jesus's birth changed everything, for He is the "light of the world." He still today brings light to all who call on him.

Oftentimes when we are hurting, we escape into ourselves, right into our man-made caves. When we find ourselves in darkness, light seems impossible to see. I do believe that there is treasure to be found in darkness. One of the ways God makes us certain of His light is by allowing us to test it in the darkness. God sometimes allows things to get dark in our lives in order to develop us and teach us about Himself so we can grow our faith. Unless we find ourselves in the dark, we will not learn how to depend on God and to experience His presence. "I will give you hidden treasures, riches stored in secret places, so that you may know that I am the LORD, the God of Israel, who summons you by name" (Isa. 45:3).

How can we ever imagine that, in our deepest despair, we are lifting our hands in praise? Despair and praise don't relate to each other, right? What is despair? When I think of despair, I think of hopelessness. Webster's Dictionary 1913 defines despair as "to give up as beyond hope or expectation; to despair of."

"I waited patiently for the LORD; he turned to me and heard my cry. He lifted me out of the slimy pit, out of the mud and mire; he set my feet on a rock and gave me a firm place to stand. He put a new song in my mouth, a hymn of praise to our God. Many will see and fear the LORD and put their trust in him" (Ps. 40:1–3).

God delivered David from his enemies on multiple occasions. David had to do something first though. Can you recognize what that is? He had to wait patiently. Even after he cried out to God, he had to wait. How many of you want it now? Who me? Wait? God heard David's cries and delivered him in a powerful way. David's world changed from darkness and desperation to one of hope. And how many of us in our darkest moments fail to cry out to God and never experience the hope that God provides? I challenge you today to cry out to God. You don't need to cry out too loud because He is already right there waiting to hear from you!

David found himself many times in danger. Remember that man Saul, his cantankerous enemy who sought his life? In this particular psalm, David is praising God for His deliverance after a very fearful time. I'm challenging you today to imagine for a moment, if you will, that not just after deliverance that you might praise God. But you might praise God in the midst of the situation. I'm speaking about something that goes against the very nature of being a human being. We long for peace, comfort, happiness, and prosperity, and if we don't have that, we can't possibly praise God. If something is threatening our reality, we most certainly cannot praise God. I challenge you to begin to see things in light of God's perspective.

We all find ourselves at times in darkness. I woke up one Monday morning feeling in a very dark place. This thought became a sinking feeling of despair. How many of you know what I mean by that? It is a heaviness that, if it stays, you are sure you will not survive. God took me to a place of despair to show me how to praise Him, even with the same circumstance, and that I might share this with you.

So I ask you this question: How do we praise God when we are in this place? I mean, something has happened that has sent us into ourselves, to hopelessness and darkness. How can we sing when we feel this way? "Now faith is confidence in what we hope for and assurance about what we do not see" (Heb. 11:1). God tells us to have faith in what is unseen, not seen. That faith is the substance of things hoped for, the evidence of things unseen. Isn't hope just that? That which we can't see, but which we will see?

I'm speaking of praising God in the dark times of life. When you get fired from your job or you have no job, yet you still praise Him. I'm taking about someone hating you and wanting to destroy you, yet you praise God. I'm taking about suffering, loss and heartache, yet you praise Him. How is this possible? How is this possible when you have become the epitome of despair? When you feel so low, you simply cannot continue with this burden, heartache, and pain. That day I said, "Lord, I cannot go on unless you do something."

Do you see the change here? I went from attempting to change my situation to one of "Lord, I cannot go on unless you do something." How many of you know that when you come to the end of yourself, that is when God shows up to save the day? While He may not change the circumstance, He will give you the grace you need. Sometimes He is just waiting for you to get to this place so He can reveal His glory. This just might be your day for a miracle.

I am going to get real with you today and challenge you even further. Since you now are thinking it might be possible to praise God when you are in a despairing situation, I will share a little secret. Recently I found myself so down and out that I missed a simple truth that is found in the following scripture, "Enter his gates with thanksgiving and his courts with praise" (Ps. 100:4). I realized that my attitude was bad. I was focusing on all the negative of my situation and failed to look at my blessings.

I was struggling, but God was patient with me and He wanted me to get this simple truth. God is so full of surprises about how and where He might show up to teach you a truth. He brought a lady at a grocery store at a deli line to share a few words for me to get this point. How many of you simply hate standing in the deli line? It is one thing I dread. It was Sunday evening, and I had to pick up a couple items at the grocery.

Unexpectedly, this dear woman started sharing how she had the Sunday blues, as she was feeling a little down about the upcoming workweek. Just hearing her say that reminded me of the many times I too had that sinking feeling. Currently I was in between work so I thought how blessed I was not to have to feel that way today. It made me see my blessing. And from that blessing, I saw another and then another. And before I knew it, I was singing praises to God.

I surprised myself and had to stop and pray, "Lord, how did I get to the praise?" The simple answer is that I began to recognize the light around me, all of the blessings that God has given me. Even if my life weren't a field of daisies, He was working. I could not see it because my focus was on the darkness. I challenge you to begin to list the things you are thankful for on a daily basis.

Make a decision that you will praise God, no matter what your circumstances are. Just as you must choose what to wear each day, it is a decision to put on praise. With practice, I believe we can begin to praise God no matter what is going on around us. With this said, along with this little tip, fresh from the deli, I am going to share more tips to help you to get your praise on.

Today I want to take that thought and bring it into the reality of our personal despair, dark times in our own lives. We will only get this when we relate this to our lives. Then I'll explain how Jesus, the light of the world, disburses the darkness, enabling us to have joy and trust in God's power and sovereignty.

I've already shared how giving thanks to God leads to praising Him. Finally I'll share how something unexpected and sometimes defies logic just shows up. Grace. Yes, God's grace is even in the midst of our despair and darkness. That is possible, and we can replace our spirit of despair with a garment of praise.

God wants us to exalt Him and not our problems. It means you are saying, "Although I have these problems, I know that you, Lord, are greater than them. You are my heavenly Father, and you are good. In you, I have everything I need in life, and I choose to exalt you!" God says, **"all things God works for the good of those who love him"** (Romans 8:28). This doesn't mean it feels good. It means that God will take the pain and turn it for good if you surrender to His purposes and plan. God uses bad things sometimes to make us stronger and more like Christ. But we have to surrender to His purpose and plan. "I have come into the world as a light, so that no one who believes in me should stay in darkness" (John 12:46).

God can use a wounding to bring a healing. I am here to testify that God renews, restores, and heals through our personal heartache. Sometimes God allows suffering and brokenness to bring us closer to His heart and to make us more like Christ. God is the light in the darkness. Sometimes we fear losing control, but He is right there when we finally surrender and let go. God is good even when He is not understood. God is always faithful.

I once heard a story that stuck with me. I believe it relates to what I am sharing. A father was with his son who needed stitches. As they were in the emergency room, he held his son's face and said, "Look at me. This pain is necessary so there will be a better ending to the story. Trust me. Just keep looking at me, and I am here with you to get you through it."

I'm challenging you today to recognize that the difficult times, the challenging times, and the darkest of times can actually lead to finding beautiful lights shimmering in the darkness. God can take the brokenness, the pain, and the sorrow and use it to redeem, restore, and heal you. And He can use it to do the same to those who are watching from the sidelines. Jesus is the light of the world. Jesus, the light of the world, turns our darkness into light, which leads us to have great joy as we encounter God's power and His great sovereignty in all things.

> As he went along, he saw a man blind from birth. His disciples asked him, "Rabbi, who sinned, this man or his parents, that he was born blind?" "Neither this man nor his parents sinned," said Jesus, "but this happened so that the works of God might be displayed in him. As long as it is day, we must do the works of him who sent me. Night is coming, when no one can work. While I am in the world, I am the light of the world" (John 9:1–5).

Jesus soon heals the blind man to show mankind the love and purposes of God. This great miracle would reveal God's glory. This miracle would prove that Jesus is the light of the world.

I believe this same God is still in the business of miracles and providing signs that he is indeed the light of the world. So if you need a miracle in your dark situation, do not give up. I believe God can and does perform miracles today. And while God may or may not choose to do a miracle in your particular dark situation, He shows up in many ways to lighten your darkness. You just have to seek Him. There are many scriptures in the Bible where God does this. He delivers and gives strength. We all need hope when we find ourselves in the darkness. Here are some ways:

- God shows scriptures to us often during these times as promises. We feel a quickening in our spirit that was, for me, this particular issue.
- After surrendering an issue, we all of a sudden feel peace that defies logic. This is grace. And we go on, but this time, we are not torn up inside.

These often provide the encouragement and courage to continue a difficult journey. Can you think of others?

I am an avid believer in the power of scriptures to change a life. Please reflect on these two scriptures of hope. One thing I have found helpful is to write scriptures that are meaningful to you on note cards and place them where you will see them as reminders of God's great love and promises to you.

- "This is what the LORD says: 'In the time of my favor I will answer you, and in the day of salvation I will help you; to be a covenant for the people, to restore the land and to reassign its desolate inheritances, to say to the captives, 'Come out,' and to those in darkness, 'Be free!' They will feed beside the roads and find pasture on every barren hill'" (Isa. 49:8–9).
- "Enter his gates with thanksgiving and his courts with praise; give thanks to him and praise his name" (Ps. 100:4).

So imagine with me that you are entering His gates with thanksgiving and into His courts with praise. We put on the garment of praise, and as we praise Him, our spirits are lifted. "Why, my soul, are you downcast? Why so disturbed within me? Put your hope in God, for I will yet praise him, my Savior and my God" (Ps. 42:5).

David found the secret to hopelessness, the hopelessness of which I described that had trickled into my heart and mind and sent me into a rushing current of despair. David encouraged his soul to praise God. He made a decision to recognize God's characteristics despite his feelings of despair. When we choose to dwell upon God's character, we always have something to praise him for, His unfailing love, mercy, kindness, goodness, and power. When we want to increase our hope, we can start praising. By having a close relationship with the Lord, we will increase our joy. If you are in deep pain, sorrow, despair, or confusion, encourage yourself to praise God.

I testify that grace is real and has changed my life. If anyone were to ask me to define grace, I would say the following. Grace is the unmerited favor of God toward us in that, while we were sinners, Christ died for us. And nothing but grace, not even our works, saves us. Second, grace is strength that shows up for the journey.

Grace showed up for me one afternoon after I had fallen to my knees in tears over an uncontrollable matter in my life. This matter had left me without peace for several years. After this day, I had a peace that passes understanding even though nothing in the situation had changed. For me in the difficult journey, it was the promise I received from God. God gave me scriptures and spoke to me, providing a peace that He would be faithful in the circumstance. He asked only that I give the burden to Him to carry and that I not carry it myself.

Every difficult situation is an opportunity to grow in trusting God. The external situations and circumstances reveal what is in our heart. Are we putting our hope in God? Where is our hope? When I find myself tangled up in worry, fear, or control, I need to take a chill pill and ask myself this question: What lie am I believing about the characteristics of God, or have I forgotten His characteristics? So I challenge you in the dark times to come to a place of absolute surrender of this matter to God. Share with God your thoughts and feelings on the situation and rest in His promises and characteristics. What are God's characteristics?

Psalm 103 reveals many of God's characteristics, and it is a model for praying during times of despair. David wrote this psalm as a reflection of the Lord's holy character. We also can pray it during our times of despair. Let's read it and offer it as a prayer to the Lord in our dark times. Will you take a moment to reflect on these characteristics and determine how they apply to your current situation?

Praise the LORD, my soul; all my inmost being, praise his holy name. Praise the LORD, my soul, and forget not all his benefits—who forgives all your sins and heals all your diseases, who redeems your life from the pit and crowns you with love and compassion, who satisfies your desires with good things so that your youth is renewed like the eagle's.

The LORD works righteousness and justice for all the oppressed. He made known his ways to Moses, his deeds to the people of Israel: The LORD is compassionate and gracious, slow to anger, abounding in love. He will not always accuse, nor will he harbor his anger forever; he does not treat us as our sins deserve or repay us according to our iniquities. For as high as the heavens are above the earth, so great is his love for those who fear him; as far as the east is from the west, so far has he removed our transgressions from us. As a father has compassion on his children, so the LORD has compassion on those who fear him; for he knows how we are formed,

he remembers that we are dust. The life of mortals is like grass, they flourish like a flower of the field; the wind blows over it and it is gone, and its place remembers it no more. But from everlasting to everlasting the LORD's love is with those who fear him, and his righteousness with their children's children—with those who keep his covenant and remember to obey his precepts. The LORD has established his throne in heaven, and his kingdom rules over all. Praise the LORD, you his angels, you mighty ones who do his bidding, who obey his word. Praise the LORD, all his heavenly hosts, you his servants who do his will. Praise the LORD, all his works everywhere in his dominion. Praise the LORD, my soul.

"But you are a chosen people, a royal priesthood, a holy nation, God's special possession, that you may declare the praises of him who called you out of darkness into his wonderful light" (1 Pet. 2:9).

CHAPTER 4

What Are You Hoping For?

We all love gifts. What is it about receiving a gift that excites us so much? Is it the element of surprise or the excitement of receiving something shiny and new? Is it possible that we can treasure these gifts in our hearts and allow them to be our hope? I challenge you today to imagine that the gifts and blessings that of course come from the Lord actually can become our source of hope. You ask, "How can that be?"

If you were to receive a gift today, what would you hope for? Let's go deeper: What is the cry of your soul? I am not talking about something you want. I am talking about something you cherish and treasure, an object that gives you a physical ache in your chest at the thought of not having it. I am talking about the heart-wrenching situations, the ones that keep you up at night. What are you hoping for?

Are you broken, suffering, or longing to touch the hem of His garment as the woman with the issue of blood of whom Jesus healed? Are you out of luck, out of sorts, or desperate for hope? Are you in despair about to give up? Are you wondering how anything beautiful can come out of the ashes of your life? Of all the horrible things that others have done to you, what hope can come out of our meekness, our mourning, or our weakness and fear?

And what about hope? Have you seen any glimmer of hope in the situation of which we are describing? Have you felt a glimpse of hope at the first sign of an answered prayer? Have you wanted something so badly that you can taste it? Are you searching for hope today? And what is hope? Webster's 1913 defines hope as "to place confidence; to trust with confident expectation of good; usually followed by in."

It was a cloudy day on the coast. The weather experts were predicting when and where Hurricane Matthew might hit and telling us how to prepare. On my shopping list that day was water, water, and more water. As I went to purchase water, all of the stores were out of water. I began to worry. You know what? I did find water that day. The Lord in His mercy did provide water. It was a journey of searching, but the Lord provided. How many of us do not place water on our personal lists, although it is the one thing that we most desperately need. I am speaking of the living water, Jesus.

In contrast (and as I read the news headlines that day), it seemed every story was about tragedy and loss. And I thought to myself, *Most of the time before the personal storms hit, there are no warnings, no planning, and no preparation. We are blindsided.* Just like this approaching storm, we can do all we can to protect life and property, but ultimately things can still happen because we live in a fallen world.

I share this because we have two choices when tragedy strikes. We can sink into despair and depression, or we can choose to trust and believe in a mighty God who has promised to take our hand, to never leave or forsake us, and to walk with us through whatever our journey changes into or looks like. God is a God of hope, our very present help in times of trouble and a strong tower. Yes, life is difficult. However, you are not meant to carry the burdens that life hands you at times. You are asked to surrender your burdens to the Lord and to journey to new life.

Just like this hurricane, as we are in the midst of the trauma and the devastation, it is almost impossible to look beyond the moment. I remember in my journey when I lost my mom in a tragic car accident. I was angry with God. Often the only safe place to take out our anger is with God. However, what I learned in retrospect is that God did not cause the accident. Nor was He not aware or uncaring about my hurt. I learned, in retrospect, that God was with me the entire time. When you are angry, say so, and it is okay to tell God how you feel. He is a big God and can take it. But ultimately God loves you, and He has promised to be with you in whatever you face in this journey called life.

As I was driving through the roads of devastated North Carolina, I noticed a sign at a church that read, "Are you looking for the blessed hope?" And so I ask you: what are you hoping for? Our only hope in this life is our Lord and Savior Jesus Christ. He is holding out His hand for you. Will you take it?

My friend, God is turning it all around. Yes, He is restoring and giving us all the enemy took. Put your hope in Him! I had a really stressful home life when I was growing up, and one thing I remember was looking forward to the day when things would be better. As a small child, God began planting a seed of hope in me that he continues to use to give hope to others. I share this so you can be encouraged that, if you are in a bad circumstance right now, my friend, it will not always be this way! Put your hope in God. "Why, my soul, are you downcast? Why so disturbed within me? Put your hope in God, for I will yet praise him, my Savior and my God" (Ps. 43:5).

God is the reason we can have hope. The history of Israel shows again and again that our way does not work. We cannot achieve God's purposes by our human strength, reason, or ability. God simply does not do things the way we think, and His ways are not our own. Our ways and efforts can often get messed up. We think in terms of material things, objects we can see, our strength, and our ability, all things of this world. But God thinks in terms of tiny beginnings, of spiritual rather than physical strength, and of victory in weakness, not in terms of human ambition. God's economy is upside down from the world's economy. The way up is down. I have had to learn this principle over and over because, by nature, I am a planner and a visionary leader.

Don't miss the hope because you are looking for it in shiny, beautiful things or under ribbons and bows. Jesus represents hope. When Jesus was born, the Jewish nation was in difficult times, looking pretty hopeless. There were no great signs of hope and deliverance from difficulty. There was no sign except that a virgin had conceived and given birth, an indication that no one in Nazareth or Judah would believe. Hope is found in humble beginnings, brokenness, desperation, shepherds, poor Jewish girls, mourning, or brokenness. Please don't miss Him at His second coming as those missed Him at His first coming.

Look up! Your redemption draws nigh! But he gives us more grace. That is why Scripture says, "God opposes the proud but shows favor to the humble" (James 4:6).

Has God ever given you a promise that a situation would turn around? You are so excited, but as time goes on, you start getting weary because it hasn't happened as quickly as you had imagined it would? Have you ever hoped for something, but it took a long time for you to see it? Hope deferred is difficult because, as we long for the hope of the promise delivered or whatever, we get caught up in the human time zone, as I call it. We want it now.

But, my friend, this is when God's grace shows up as we release the situation to Jesus. These times are when the grace of God carries us, the grace that the angels longed to look into and grace that God gives to the humble, as stated in James 4:6. And in God's timing, the day of salvation will arrive. Hope is not defined by the kingdom of the earth; it's defined by the kingdom of God. "Glory to God in the highest heaven, and on earth peace to those on whom his favor rests" (Luke 2:14).

Favor! What does this have to do with favor? I'm here to testify that the favor of God rests on the humble in spirit—the surrendered, meek, teachable heart; the broken, desperate for hope; the downcast in Spirit; the ones who walk in relationship with God and set their hope in him; the ones who Paul says, "May the God of hope fill you with all joy and peace as you trust in him, so that you may overflow with hope by the power of the Holy Spirit" (Rom. 15:13). Through endurance and encouragement of the scriptures, we have hope. Life is hard, but we have Hope if we look for it in God.

As I was walking my journey, God began reminding me of hope. On four occasions, I saw reminders of hope. The first was a scripture.

> This is what the LORD says: "In the time of my favor I will answer you, and in the day of salvation I will help you; I will keep you and will make you to be a covenant for the people, to restore the land and to reassign its desolate inheritances, to say to the captives, 'Come out,'

and to those in darkness, 'Be free!' They will feed beside the roads and find pasture on every barren hill" (Isa. 49:8–9).

The second reminder He gave me occurred on the same day as above. "As God's coworkers, we urge you not to receive God's grace in vain. For he says, "In the time of my favor I heard you, and in the day of salvation I helped you" (2 Corinthians 6:1-2).

I tell you that now is the time of God's favor. "Now is the day of salvation" (2 Cor. 6:2). This promise was given again, the same promise from two scriptures. It's not a coincidence. How many of you know that there are no coincidences in God's economy? God was emphasizing hope to me when I needed it the most.

Finally God gave me this promise the fourth time when He gave me Isaiah 49:8–9 again. I believe that God in His love wants to toss out reminders in different ways. We just have to be willing to listen. I shared this to remind you that hope can be found all around you. You just have to be looking and listening.

We experience hope when we are broken. Jesus said, "Blessed are the Poor in Spirit, for theirs is the Kingdom of Heaven" (Matt. 5:3). We must admit that we are in need of help. This means admitting that we need God and then depending on Him. We are blessed when we are at the end of our rope. With less of us, there is more of God's rule. We are blessed when we mourn because we will be comforted. "Blessed are those that mourn, for they will be comforted" (Matt. 5:4). This comfort comes from knowing that Immanuel God is with us and comforts us in our time of need. We are blessed when we are meek. "Blessed are the meek, for they will inherit the earth" (Matt. 5:5).

Webster's Dictionary 1913 defines meek as "mild of temper; not easily provoked or irritated; patient under injuries; not vain, or haughty, or resentful; forbearing; submissive." We can only receive this with God's help. If we want to possess meekness, we must be willing to surrender and trust in God's plans and purposes.

Don't miss hope because it doesn't come wrapped in pretty ribbons and paper! Hope is not found in circumstances, happiness, money, careers, and relationships. Hope is found in the unexpected, a baby wrapped in swaddling clothing in a dirty manger to the most unlikely, poor Jewish parents. Most will miss Jesus in this day just as they missed Him on that dark starry night. "This will be a sign to you: You will find a baby wrapped in cloths and lying in a manger" (Luke 2:12). The baby Jesus was and is the world's only hope for peace and meaning in life. Don't miss Him at His second coming. At your time of great trouble, don't miss His hand and His control in what you are experiencing. Place your hope in the Lord Jesus Christ, the Messiah, the promised one, the one who promises this,

> To bind up the brokenhearted, to proclaim freedom for the captives and release from darkness for the prisoners, to proclaim the year of the LORD's favor and the day of vengeance of our God, to comfort all who mourn, and provide for those who grieve in Zion—to bestow on them a crown of beauty instead of ashes, the oil of joy instead of mourning, and a garment of praise instead of a spirit of despair" (Isa. 61:1–3).

What promise has God made to you, and yet years have gone by and nothing seems to have changed or happened as God promised? Are you out on a limb, having obediently followed the Lord's instruction, yet others look at you as if you are foolish? "For to us a child is born, to us a son is given, and the government will be on his shoulders. And he will be called Wonderful Counselor, Mighty God, Everlasting Father, Prince of Peace" (Isa. 9:6).

Isaiah prophesized the birth of the Messiah, the one who would finally deliver hope. A period of seven hundred years went by before this prophecy was fulfilled—seven hundred years of frustrated hope, sin, wandering, hope deferred, and struggles like today, however with no hope. We are different. We now have hope. Jesus is alive and is our hope.

Are you feeling alone in your suffering with no one to understand? In the Bible, a man named Job lost everything, and even his wife told him to curse God and die. Can you relate to this man? He cried out to God for understanding of his suffering. He wrestled with God and attempted to put human reasoning into his experience of suffering. And guess what? From this questioning, he gained an understanding that God's ways are not our ways. However, may I offer hope in our suffering because when we are in the midst of suffering and we are allowed to feel the presence of God in our suffering, it may be bittersweet, but we begin to realize that what we go through has purpose. And, may I add that we now have a High Priest that understands our sufferings. This is because of Jesus's work on the cross. He was the suffering servant. When Jesus died on the cross, the veil in the Holy of Holies was torn. God reconciled Himself with man, and now we can come boldly before the throne of God in our time of need. Grace and hope are found in Jesus. "May the God of hope fill you with all joy and peace as you trust in him, so that you may overflow with hope by the power of the Holy Spirit" (Rom. 15:13).

There is something joyful about a message directed specifically to us. When taken to a personal level, it brings joy. I am here to testify that Jesus was born for you, to bring you hope—specifically eternal hope, grace, and power in the situations in your life—to give you freedom from any captivity in your life, and to bring deliverance and a new beginning. Joy to you!

In the story of the birth of Jesus, Mary was visited by the angel Gabriel, who shared with her that she was favored to be the one to give birth to Jesus, the Messiah. "The angel answered, 'The Holy Spirit will come on you, and the power of the Most High will overshadow you. So the holy one to be born will be called the Son of God'" (Luke 1:35).

Can you imagine the joy experienced knowing this message was for her personally? I am here to testify that God wants to share with you a personal message that will bring you joy in your circumstance! He did for me, and He will do for you. God's promises always come true. Hold onto these words in your heart, even if they are for a future time! They bring great hope in dark times.

How many of you have received a word from the Lord, a promise, and then you meet another who tells you exactly what you heard from the Lord? Or unexpectedly, a coincidence happens that you know was a confirmation from God. God wants you to experience joy in your life at the promises He will deliver, the situations and battles that He will fight for you. It's the victories. After one touch of His hand, your situation will change. Joy to the world! The Lord has come. God receives glory through giving us joy, delivering us, and providing grace.

Jesus came as a baby in a manger in a humble way, but let me tell you, "Jesus is the lion of Judah, and with His power, He will fight for you." In Exodus 14, we read the story of Moses as he led the Israelites. Here is the scene I want you to see. It is the scene of the Exodus, and Moses is leading the Israelites away from captivity. Even though Pharaoh released the people, he soon regrets and fears that the release also meant the loss of their services to him. So he gets together a huge army, six hundred of the best chariots plus all of the chariots of Egypt. He sets out after the Israelites. It looked like all was lost. The enemy had won. They cried out to Moses in fear that they had been taken out in the desert to die, that God had forsaken them, and that they were toast.

By man, it looked impossible. They were cornered at the edge of the Red Sea. Have you ever felt like that? Do you feel that your enemy is too powerful? Too strong? That things are hopeless and too big to handle? That you are better off in bondage? That you deserve this? That this is your plight? Or that being alone, starting over, or fleeing from your enemy is too impossible? That abuse is comfortable so you stay? And over and over, you try your best to save yourself! Please hang on and listen to the following scripture.

> Moses answered the people, "Do not be afraid. Stand firm and you will see the deliverance the LORD will bring you today. The Egyptians you see today you will never see again. The LORD will fight for you; you need only to be still." Then the LORD said to Moses, "Why are you crying out to me? Tell the Israelites to move on. Raise your staff and stretch out your hand over the sea to divide the water so that the Israelites can go through the sea on dry ground. I will harden the hearts of the Egyptians so that they will go in after them. And I will

gain glory through Pharaoh and all his army, through his chariots and his horsemen. The Egyptians will know that I am the LORD when I gain glory through Pharaoh, his chariots and his horsemen." Then the angel of God, who had been traveling in front of Israel's army, withdrew and went behind them. The pillar of cloud also moved from in front and stood behind them, coming between the armies of Egypt and Israel. Throughout the night the cloud brought darkness to the one side and light to the other side; so neither went near the other all night long. Then Moses stretched out his hand over the sea, and all that night the LORD drove the sea back with a strong east wind and turned it into dry land. The waters were divided, and the Israelites went through the sea on dry ground, with a wall of water on their right and on their left. The Egyptians pursued them, and all Pharaoh's horses and chariots and horsemen followed them into the sea. During the last watch of the night the LORD looked down from the pillar of fire and cloud at the Egyptian army and threw it into confusion. He jammed the wheels of their chariots so that they had difficulty driving. And the Egyptians said, "Let's get away from the Israelites! The LORD is fighting for them against Egypt." Then the LORD said to Moses, "Stretch out your hand over the sea so that the waters may flow back over the Egyptians and their chariots and horsemen." Moses stretched out his hand over the sea, and at daybreak the sea went back to its place. The Egyptians were fleeing toward it, and the LORD swept them into the sea. The water flowed back and covered the chariots and horsemen—the entire army of Pharaoh that had followed the Israelites into the sea. Not one of them survived. But the Israelites went through the sea on dry ground, with a wall of water on their right and on their left. That day the LORD saved Israel from the hands of the Egyptians, and Israel saw the Egyptians lying dead on the shore. And when the Israelites saw the mighty hand of the LORD displayed against the Egyptians, the people feared the LORD and put their trust in him and in Moses his servant (Ex. 14:13–31).

But after this great miracle, remember how they grumbled, feared, and didn't trust God's promises? Remember how God then allowed them to wander in the wilderness for forty years and not enter the Promised Land? Please don't miss this point. God is about to take you into your Promised Land, but you must surrender and trust Him with your situation. He is mighty to save! Give your situation to God! "But those who hope in the LORD will renew their strength. They will soar on wings like eagles; they will run and not grow weary, they will walk and not be faint" (Isa. 40:31).

All things are possible with God. "Jesus looked at them and said, "With man this is impossible, but with God all things are possible" (Matt. 19:26).

Have you ever felt a deep yearning for hope in your circumstances? Has God given you a promise, yet years go by and you do not see it? The story of Joseph in the book of Genesis is a great story of hope. Joseph was asked to do something that most could never do. However, Joseph faithfully followed God. God took Joseph on a path paved with fear, uncertainty, threats and danger, physical discomfort, and pain. Yet through all of this, Joseph trusted God that He would be faithful to His promises. Joseph knew that, at the end of all of the sorrow and suffering, hope would arise. Can we let our faith arise in our difficult times? Can we trust that God will faithfully carry us in our trials and fulfill His promises—even as Joseph did—when everything around us appears that this is not true? Can we turn to Him and trust Him to carry us and to give us peace and grace? "Let us hold unswervingly to the hope we profess, for he who promised is faithful" (Heb. 10:23). God made a promise to Joseph, and He ultimately fulfilled it.

Ultimately, can we truly understand or desire to understand that the one who hung the stars and set the earth in motion is the Great I Am, the Alpha, and the Omega? He is the one who can do anything. God loves to give us joy. My friend, God wants to do the same for you. He sent His one and only Son to the world as a baby in a manger. This is a personal message for you of the joy God wants for you. He loves you and is so faithful to be here for you.

So I ask you again: are you looking for hope in pretty ribbons and bows? Fall on your knees humbly before your Savior, surrender all of your hopes and desires to Him, and hear the angel voices as they announce the birth of our Lord and Savior, the one who will turn our ashes into beauty. He is our deliverer, the Great High Priest who intercedes for us. He is the Prince of Peace, the Lord of Lords. Immanuel God is with us! Come to Jesus, the blessed hope for hope.

> But now, this is what the LORD says—he who created you, Jacob, he who formed you, Israel: "Do not fear, for I have redeemed you; I have summoned you by name; you are mine. When you pass through the waters, I will be with you; and when you pass through the rivers, they will not sweep over you. When you walk through the fire, you will not be burned; the flames will not set you ablaze. For I am the LORD your God, the Holy One of Israel, your Savior; I give Egypt for your ransom, Cush and Seba in your stead. Since you are precious and honored in my sight, and because I love you, I will give people in exchange for you, nations in exchange for your life.

> Do not be afraid, for I am with you; I will bring your children from the east and gather you from the west. I will say to the north, 'Give them up!' and to the south, 'Do not hold them back.' Bring my sons from afar and my daughters from the ends of the earth—everyone who is called by my name, whom I created for my glory, whom I formed and made." Lead out those who have eyes but are blind, who have ears but are deaf. All

the nations gather together and the peoples assemble. Which of their gods foretold this and proclaimed to us the former things? Let them bring in their witnesses to prove they were right, so that others may hear and say, "It is true." "You are my witnesses," declares the LORD, "and my servant whom I have chosen, so that you may know and believe me and understand that I am he. Before me no god was formed, nor will there be one after me. I, even I, am the LORD, and apart from me there is no savior. I have revealed and saved and proclaimed—I, and not some foreign god among you. You are my witnesses," declares the LORD, "that I am God. Yes, and from ancient days I am he. No one can deliver out of my hand. When I act, who can reverse it?" (Isa. 43:1–13).

CHAPTER 5

By His Stripes

A few years ago, I was at a conference, and as I sat there waiting, I noticed a man walking around. There were lots of people walking around, but for some reason, this man caught my attention. In my spirit, I had a strong impression that this man was hopeless. I did not know him. I had never seen him before that day. But the feeling was so strong that I jumped up and told my coworker I had to find him because he had no hope. However, as I walked the hallways of that building, I could not find him. And what if I had? What would I say? "Jesus wa—."

I have to share what just happened, not then but now. As I was starting to write the words that Jesus was his only hope, my nose started bleeding. So going back to my story, this time I made a change to my initial words that I would have shared that day with the man who had no hope. I would share that his only hope would be found in the blood of Jesus, our only hope for salvation, redemption, restoration, and healing, all of it. Wow! Thank you, Jesus. Thank you for reminding me of your blood. I must share that this is just another example of how God has been working in the writing of this book.

Anyhow, let's go back to my original story. That afternoon, in a breakout session for training, there he sat. As the speaker said the words, "hope deferred," he let out a sigh as if to release a burden he had been holding inside. While I do not fully understand why I was allowed to see this in this man that day, I do know that God and the blood of Jesus is our only hope. Joy fills me as I read those words on the page.

And now would you imagine the great joy that the disciples had when they realized that Jesus was alive? The same Jesus who shed his blood for mankind was alive. The same Jesus who was raised from the dead is alive today. Now I want you to imagine with me: could any situation be hopeless when Jesus is alive today?

This is a journey of restoration as God begins restoring all that the enemy has taken. And this journey to new life is all about the journey. When we think of taking a journey, we often focus on the destination, where we are traveling to. We overlook the journey itself. That is not what this book is all about. While hope fills this journey, ultimately it is the story of the power of the blood of the cross and how Jesus is alive today, transforming lives. It is a reminder of God's great love for you by sending His Son Jesus to die on the cross, to suffer the worst imaginable death, and to shed His blood for you and me. There had to be a perfect sacrifice and a shedding of blood for there to be a forgiveness of sin. This work, this blood of Jesus, released the power that takes our suffering and brokenness and brings healing, hope, and restoration. Our suffering and pain can turn into our healing and wholeness in Christ. Why? God's desire is for you to be restored, so when you suffer, He is right there to pick you up.

This journey is fluid and ever-changing. Have you ever watched the Weather Channel? The weather models predict where catastrophic storms may hit. Even with all of the technology of where storms may hit, oftentimes the reality is that they hit in ways not predicted. Life is like that. There are no strategic models to warn us of what we will encounter on our journey or what we encountered in our past. And as I write this, please do not miss the joy or the hope in the journey as I did. I was looking for the destination. What I realized in retrospect was the healing that happened along the way.

I can still recall where I was when I was told that my best friend, my mom, had died in a car accident. I can see the room I was in and the floor that my knees buckled upon. I can still remember the kick I felt in my gut as life as I knew it changed forever. As I bring back that day in my journey, for some reason I recall a memorable vacation to Charleston, South Carolina. It was my first time to Charleston, and I was so excited. I had my travel guide in hand and my husband, Mark by my side. As we toured this beautiful city, I was drawn to a row of houses called Rainbow Row. Like my thoughts, they seemed to appear out of nowhere.

Have you ever visited a museum and enjoyed the art? To me, I enjoy taking the time to reflect on the art, not just the piece itself, but the artist's perspective, what he or she was seeking to capture in that particular moment in time. As we walked along the street, the sun was setting, which brought out the beauty of the colors on the buildings. There is something about the evening in this holy city that catches your attention. Even with the darkness approaching, the reflections of light seem to make everything brighter. As we walked on this particular day, we were in it for the day. You know the sort of day when your feet are hurting so bad, but you just have to see one more thing.

As we walked back to our car, we passed Rainbow Row again, and this time it was completely dark. But again, there is something about the night in Charleston that is different. It seems the city comes alive at night as tourists walk the streets, enjoying the fine dining restaurants. The lights seem to shine brighter, and even in the darkness, there is such beauty.

The day I lost my mom was dark for me, but because of Jesus and the hope He gave me, there was never total darkness from the loss of my mom. I knew I would see her in heaven. Yes, I said good-bye on this earth, but I only said, "See you later." Just as the buildings of Rainbow Row were given new life at one point in time, God will do the same for you. And as I view that day through the perspective of one broken and dark day, I remember Jesus. For you see, Jesus is our only hope (light) on the dark days, and just like Rainbow Row at night, I can still see the light. Do you have a similar moment that you recall? Or is now your moment of darkness?

And so a tragedy strikes, a loss happens, a trauma hits home, and life as we know it changes forever. It is at these times that Jesus is near. He is near to the brokenhearted. "The LORD is close to the brokenhearted and saves those who are crushed in spirit" (Ps. 34:18). But the Lord is also there for hope, healing, and restoration, even in the midst of trauma, crises, and great loss.

In my life, the Holy Spirit began revealing how the power of the cross heals and transforms lives and ultimately how sharing all of the pain and opening your wounds to the healing power of the blood of Jesus brings healing to your wounds. This journey to new life is a reflection of how the Lord can take brokenness and use it as a springboard to minister to others who were devastated and broken by the pain in their lives. I pray that this book will bless you. Within this book are words that were Holy Spirit inspired and used as messages in ministry. The power of the cross is real and this book is a testimony of that power. "Ask and it will be given to you; seek and you will find; knock and the door will be opened to you" (Matt. 7:7).

The launching pad for these messages was Isaiah 61. I will start with an overview of how the messages progressed within ministry, and as we continue along in the book, we will cover each building block in more detail. "I delight greatly in the LORD; my soul rejoices in my God. For he has clothed me with garments of salvation and arrayed me in a robe of his righteousness, as a bridegroom adorns his head like a priest, and as a bride adorns herself with her jewels" (Isa. 61:10).

This promise is a scripture of hope. It is the first sequin of hope. It is to be used at the beginning. In ministry, I shared this scripture with a message that, because of the power of the cross and the work done there, when God looks at us, He sees Jesus. He sees you in a beautiful robe of righteousness. To make this truth tangible and real for the participants, the Lord led me to make it an art project, to imagine what this robe looked like. I had them design a dress or garment. God sees you as such. This is the essence of who you are. And so began the process of visualizing and imagining a personal robe of righteousness.

Next, I asked the participants to recognize any false beliefs or lies that are contrary to who God says they are, yet another sequin. Please note that at times these lies can come to light by statements made out loud or a thought that simply does not line up in agreement with who God says you are or about the situation. If this happens, ask the Lord for the theory of why you said that statement. He is faithful, and He will share with you. Journaling and sharing in the light of Jesus brings healing. Once the lie is exposed, you take the falsehood and allow the Holy Spirit to share what the thought process is that serves as fuel to the lie. Again, journaling helps. This lie is then replaced with facts that are true, God's truth and what His Word says. Ultimately and within this process, sharing all of the pain and opening your wounds to the healing power of the blood of Jesus brings healing to your wounds. Do you notice another sequin here? This lie is replaced with facts that were true, God's truth and what His Word says. Do you notice another sequin here?

Then I continued sharing messages of God's truth. I reminded each person of the fact they are in a robe of righteousness and nothing ever changes this fact. As part of this exercise with the robe of righteousness in combination with recognizing any lies you have been believing, you will begin the process of replacing these lies with truth. As you allow Jesus to heal the wounds, then the dress/garment is further solidified for you. You will finally get it and believe it from your heart, not just your head. This brings healing and solidifies the dress/garment.

At this point, I had lost count of the many sequins of hope. In addition, the Lord revealed to me the process of healing hurts that are in our hearts, sometimes from decades ago. This journey of hope, healing, and restoration is my gift to you. The rest of this book will be sharing this gift with you. My prayer is that you will find numerous sequins of hope in your own life as you read about the multiple sequins of hope in my journey.

Have you ever looked out your window on a beautiful day but knew you had a lot to do inside and would not be able to enjoy the outside that day? Sometimes we can see the joy outside our window, but inside we are caught up in the pain and hurt of our circumstance. But I am here to testify that this when you grow the most. You heal. Like a butterfly before it leaves the cocoon, you need to be still and know He is God. God is still good and sovereign. God is with you, and He will never leave you.

It is normal to not feel joy in this part of the journey. As I traveled this road to healing and new life, the Holy Spirit taught me profound things, which I did not know. The Lord allowed me to walk alongside others who were broken. The Lord made a promise that, if we call on

Him, He will tell us great and mighty things that we do not know. This journey is deeply rooted in a relationship with the Lord. I had to surrender before each breakthrough. Please keep your journal close by because the Holy Spirit just might reveal to you something needing Jesus's healing touch. Just like a gardener tends his garden, God will turn the desert of your life into a beautiful garden. Will you let Him?

And now let's return back to the star of this chapter and the entire book. How many of us walk around in darkness and don't even realize it? The light of the world, Jesus Christ, has already arrived. Jesus is alive, and His resurrection power breaks the chains of captivity and darkness from our lives. We have the hope of freedom in our lives. "So if the Son sets you free, you will be free indeed" (John 8:36). In the hard knocks of life—the abuse, the suffering, the injustice, the loss, the trauma, the shock, the emergency, the heartache, and the pain, all of it—Jesus is our only hope. He is our redeemer, the one who is our hope and redeems all of the broken places of our lives. Jesus transforms us in the journey. So will you take His hand as we journey to the cross to examine just what Jesus did for us on that day?

> Who has believed our message and to whom has the arm of the LORD been revealed? He grew up before him like a tender shoot, and like a root out of dry ground. He had no beauty or majesty to attract us to him, nothing in his appearance that we should desire him. He was despised and rejected by mankind, a man of suffering, and familiar with pain. Like one from whom people hide their faces he was despised, and we held him in low esteem. Surely he took up our pain and bore our suffering, yet we considered him punished by God, stricken by him, and afflicted. But he was pierced for our transgressions, he was crushed for our iniquities; the punishment that brought us peace was on him, and by his wounds we are healed. We all, like sheep, have gone astray, each of us has turned to our own way; and the LORD has laid on him the iniquity of us all. He

was oppressed and afflicted, yet he did not open his
mouth; he was led like a lamb to the slaughter, and as a
sheep before its shearers is silent, so he did not open his
mouth. By oppression and judgment he was taken away.
Yet who of his generation protested? For he was cut off
from the land of the living; for the transgression of my
people he was punished (Isa. 53:1–8).

"Therefore, if anyone is in Christ, the new creation has come: The
old has gone, the new is here" (2 Cor. 5:17).

This is a story of God's great love for you by sending His Son Jesus
to die on the cross, to suffer the worst imaginable death, and to shed
His blood for you and for me. There had to be a perfect sacrifice and
a shedding of blood for there to be a forgiveness of sin. This work of
the cross and the blood released the power that takes our suffering and
brokenness and brings healing, hope, and restoration. This shedding
of blood means a whole new life is offered to you. Jesus is alive. His
finished work on the cross releases the power and grace necessary to
remove the chains from your life. Jesus came to walk with you through
the pain in your heart and to carry the burdens that you were never
meant to transport. He came to offer a new beginning, a fresh start.
Once you accept Him as your personal Lord and Savior, your sins are
tossed into the sea of forgetfulness, never to be brought up again. Old
things have passed away. You get a second chance.

The Bible says, "I will greatly rejoice in the Lord, my soul shall
be joyful in my God; for he hath clothed me with the garments of
salvation, he hath covered me with the robe of righteousness, as a
bridegroom decketh himself with ornaments, and as a bride adorneth
herself with her jewels" (Isa. 61:10). The garment of salvation and robe
of righteousness are placed upon you at the moment you receive Christ.
You no longer wear condemnation, but through God's amazing grace,
you receive forgiveness of sins and eternal life.

To believe is the first step to freedom. Before we can surrender,
which is crucial to freedom, we must choose to believe. Before we
can receive the benefits of removing those chains and stepping out of

darkness into the light, we must accept Jesus as our Lord and Savior. This seals us with the Holy Spirit. Once we accept Christ, we become new in Jesus. The robe of righteousness becomes ours and is a part of who we are.

At this point, I am reminded of a powerful testimony I heard on the Internet. If you have time, please search the Internet for a Christian hip-hop artist named Lecrae. My friend, Jesus is alive! He is holding out his hand to walk the next step in your journey with you. Are you ready to reach out and take His hand?

God is working out His hope, healing, and restoration around the world. The power of Jesus is real. At church one Sunday, a testimony was shared about a woman who shared her dream/vision in which she saw herself in a filthy dress. This young woman shared how she saw a man, Jesus, sitting at the top of a hill, and she walked over to Him. After her encounter with Jesus, she saw herself in a white dress that was no longer filthy. I share this because I heard this testimony after I had already shared these Holy Spirit-inspired messages with the broken. You will soon see the importance of the dress metaphor, which had already touched the lives of the individuals of whom I ministered.

Who You Are in Christ

"Therefore, there is now no condemnation for those who are in Christ Jesus" (Rom. 8:1). Romans 8:31–39 says,

> What, then, shall we say in response to these things? If God is for us, who can be against us? He who did not spare his own Son, but gave him up for us all—how will he not also, along with him, graciously give us all things? Who will bring any charge against those whom God has chosen? It is God who justifies. Who then is the one who condemns? No one. Christ Jesus who died—more than that, who was raised to life—is at the right hand of God and is also interceding for us. Who shall separate us from the love of Christ? Shall trouble

or hardship or persecution or famine or nakedness or danger or sword? As it is written: "For your sake we face death all day long; we are considered as sheep to be slaughtered." No, in all these things we are more than conquerors through him who loved us. For I am convinced that neither death nor life, neither angels nor demons, neither the present nor the future, nor any powers, neither height nor depth, nor anything else in all creation, will be able to separate us from the love of God that is in Christ Jesus our Lord.

Isaiah 61:10 says, "I delight greatly in the LORD; my soul rejoices in my God. For he has clothed me with garments of salvation and arrayed me in a robe of his righteousness, as a bridegroom adorns his head like a priest, and as a bride adorns herself with her jewels."

This is the essence of who you are in Christ. As we continue with these messages, we will be working toward helping you to see who you are in Christ. The work of Jesus on the cross is powerful. Christ died to heal, redeem, and restore you. In the next chapter, I will cover the significance and importance of knowing you are in this robe of righteousness. As part of this, I will have you do a homework assignment. We are going to begin to create a garment of salvation, a robe of righteousness. So as you accept the assignment to design a dress or a garment, you visualize and design accordingly. The significance is that this is placed upon you when you accept Jesus as your Savior. The church is the bride of Christ, and Jesus is the Bridegroom so you see this is not a man or woman concept. It is for whosoever will.

This will be a visual aid of who you are in Christ. While it is a fun activity, there is a much deeper reason for this exercise. I want you to begin to see yourself precisely as God sees you: righteous, pure and spotless.

May I ask a question? What might cause us to not see ourselves this way? Abuse, sin, and things that are done to us create lies from the enemy. You are robed in a robe of righteousness. Nothing changes this. Things that happen to you do not define you. Nothing changes this robe. You are not defined by anything you have done or anything that has been done to you. You are pure. You are robed in a beautiful robe. That is who you are. Nothing external changes that ever! Bad things can be said about you, and awful things can happen to you, but they do not define or change who you are in Christ.

It does not matter what you've done, do, or what has been done to you! You are dressed in a robe of righteousness, which is pure. You are not defined by abuse or action done to you (remember that it is not your fault when someone hurts you); mistakes you have made; what others say about you; and what you say about you. As you accept who you are and that this robe of righteousness is who you are, you will begin to take steps toward that person.

To summarize, when you get it that who you are in Christ does not change when things are done to you and that these things do not stick to you, there is joy. As you recognize any lies that you have been believing, you will begin the process of replacing these falsehoods with truth. As you allow Jesus to heal the wounds, then the dress/garment is further solidified for you. You will finally get it and believe it from your heart, not just your head.

Now that I have shared about the upcoming dress/garment homework, do you remember the story of the woman in the white dress? Can you imagine my surprise and the affirmation I received of the hope and significance of the dress that the Lord had already shared with me to use as a ministry tool? As I was reflecting on all of this, I remembered the day I was baptized. After I got home, I went out to hang up my white dress on the clothesline so that it could dry. I recall where I was at that time when Jesus showed up in my life. God found me in a broken place, a home filled with anger, rage, hurt, and deep pain. Jesus carried me through the distress I experienced. If it weren't for my youth group, I am not sure where I would be right now.

Stay with me here. If God can redeem my life, He can do the same for yours. Won't you join me as we place the crowns upon our heads and dance? Get ready. While you might not be ready to dance today, I envision you dancing around in your magnificent dress or garment with your crown restored upon your head.

CHAPTER 6

Robe of Righteousness

"Instead of your shame you will receive a double portion, and instead of disgrace you will rejoice in your inheritance. And so you will inherit a double portion in your land, and everlasting joy will be yours" (Isa. 61:7).

It was a beautiful sunny day as Mark and I headed out to look at property. One of the properties was a small house. As we entered the humble abode, the warmth of the sunlight dissipated from my soul. The unkempt home left me feeling uninvited. I immediately noticed that someone had placed very dark drapes over all of the windows. This created a completely dark space where absolutely no sunlight could enter.

Is it possible that the pain in our hearts can cover our lives like a curtain blocks out the light on a beautiful day? The curtains do not change the fact that the day is sunny, just like the pain does not change the fact that the joy and the beauty are there. Even when a storm is raging, the sand on Isle of Palms still has the sparkles of silver in it. My favorite scripture is the following, "Trust in the LORD with all your heart and lean not on your own understanding; in all your ways submit to him, and he will make your paths straight" (Prov. 3:5–6).

The heart is our mind, will, and emotions. We have to allow God's light to shine on our heart. We have to be willing to share our pain and open our wounds to Jesus's healing light. We have to be willing to bring everything to His light. And in doing so, His healing touches the recesses of our heart and transforms our lives. Will you allow His light to shine on your heart? We will be discussing the heart a lot in the next chapters. The Bible has a lot to say about the heart. Three scriptures come to mind as I write these words:

- "Above all else, guard your heart, for everything you do flows from it" (Prov. 4:23).
- "The heart is deceitful above all things and beyond cure. Who can understand it?" (Jer. 17:9).
- "The crucible for silver and the furnace for gold, but the LORD tests the Heart" (Prov. 17:3).

Trust in the Lord with all of your heart. For me, this statement resonates the word "surrender." Are you willing to allow Jesus to access and touch the deepest places in your heart, those places where hurt, pain, and grief may reside? This is a choice.

In addition, we must choose to claim the promises of God. "God keeps His promises always!" I came across a bracelet that says this very thing, and I found it lying in such a way that I would notice it. As we have discussed, God wants you to remember His character and His promises, which are in the Word of God. And they also are in the promises that God has given personally to you, and only you know what those personal promises are. And, like me today, they may be found as little reminders etched on bracelets.

At this time in my life, I have three promises that God has given me. While the circumstances look like these promises have not happened, I choose to believe God, and this provides me with great hope. And isn't faith the substance of things hoped for, the evidence of things unseen? Even as I write this week, one of these promises that God made to me began to bloom like a beautiful rose. Something I have prayed about for many years is happening. I feel joy as I write these words. God always fulfills His promises. And so you see, God made a promise to me. I chose to believe. Time has gone by, and I had to be patient. Now the dry desert is beginning to bloom.

Have you ever heard the cliché, "It is always darkest right before dawn"? Well, I can attest that this is a true statement. Will you open up the curtains of your heart so the light of Jesus can touch your most painful memories? Before Jesus can do His healing work, you must make a choice. Will you surrender your heart and your pain? Will you share all of it?

For me, I journaled, cried, and shared my deepest hurt and pain with Jesus. And guess what? He understands our deepest pain because He was the suffering servant. Through this, my wounds were healed. Will you begin to open up your hearts and give the burden you were never meant to carry to the one who is the Great I Am?

Life can be difficult. As a child, I grew up in an environment where unacceptable things were happening. From this, I carried a lot of shame. Though it wasn't my actions, it was transferred onto me. The same thing happens when a person harms us physically or verbally (abuse). We can walk away shamed and feeling that the abuse somehow made us bad in some way. We can even feel as if we caused the hurt or deserved it. We feel it is our fault, and we are tainted or bad. There is the shame. This happens because we are operating with lies from the enemy and away from the truth of who God says we are. Does this make sense?

How many of us have head knowledge, things we have heard and learned about who we are in Christ? But somewhere in the mess of life, the head knowledge doesn't reach the heart. And as a result, we walk around defeated and afraid, feeling like a victim. We are filled with self-blame and even loathe ourselves. Sure, we say Jesus loves me, but something is missing. Most of the time, we find ourselves walking around with shame written all over us. We are never good enough, smart enough, or talented enough. We see through the mirror of self-doubt, self-blame, and self-defeat. If only we could believe who God says we are in His Word. The Lord took me on a journey to realize this fact, and I want to share how He worked in my life.

As we journey into the next chapters, I will continue introducing you to the power of the cross and who you are in Christ. I will show you how deep hurts in life can hinder you from moving this head knowledge to heart knowledge. I will explain how Jesus takes the broken places of our lives and turns them into something beautiful. But you must be willing to open the curtains to your heart and release to Jesus all of the hurt and the pain, all of it. You were never meant to walk around defeated or to carry these burdens. During this part of the journey, keep your journal handy because you never know when your fitting for your beautiful dress or garment might show up on the calendar.

In this chapter, it is my sincere desire that you will begin visualizing who you really are, robed in this beautiful dress or garment, however you wish to visualize it. My hope is that you will begin to realize your real identity in Christ. You will experience restoration to the degree that you open up the curtains of your heart and allow the healing power of the blood of Jesus to shine on and to bring healing to your wounds. Are you ready to allow the one who was wounded to bring you healing?

"But he was pierced for our transgressions, he was crushed for our iniquities; the punishment that brought us peace was on him, and by his wounds we are healed" (Isa. 53:5).

This is about a personal relationship, one with open sharing, not a magic formula. My journey through pain is going to lead us to something so amazing that I can hardly hold back from telling you how this all ends. Oh, wait! First, a wedding is about to start. What is it about a wedding that brings such joy? For me, when I think of a wedding, I think of the following words: hope, joy, and new life. Do any of these words ring a bell?

In Isaiah 61:10, Christ's righteousness is compared to a robe, one which is as a bride and groom's attire at a wedding. "I delight greatly in the Lord; my soul rejoices in my God. For he has clothed me with garments of salvation and arrayed me in a robe of his righteousness, as a bridegroom adorns his head like a priest, and as a bride adorns herself with her jewels" (Isa. 61:10).

Look at the reference to male. Have you ever seen a groom's hair unkempt and his face unshaven on his wedding day? No, the groom ensures he looks his best for the bride. In a priestly manner, the bridegroom adorns himself.

Look at the reference to female. As a little girl, do you remember dressing up and putting on your mother's jewelry? When you did that, you really felt decked out, didn't you? In order to dress up, the bride puts on jewelry.

This scripture also describes Christ as the Bridegroom and all people as believers. Both male and female are referred to as the "bride." It is my belief that the following scriptures reflect in a very real way just how God loves you. Words are powerful, and I truly believe that there is indeed life and death in the power of the tongue. "Therefore, there is now no condemnation for those who are in Christ Jesus" (Rom. 8:1). Romans 8:31–39 says,

> What, then, shall we say in response to these things? If God is for us, who can be against us? He who did not spare his own Son, but gave him up for us all—how will he not also, along with him, graciously give us all things? Who will bring any charge against those whom God has chosen? It is God who justifies. Who then is the one who condemns? No one. Christ Jesus who died—more than that, who was raised to life—is at the right hand of God and is also interceding for us. Who shall separate us from the love of Christ? Shall trouble or hardship or persecution or famine or nakedness or danger or sword? As it is written: "For your sake we face death all day long; we are considered as sheep to be slaughtered." No, in all these things we are more than conquerors through him who loved us. For I am convinced that neither death nor life, neither angels nor demons, neither the present nor the future, nor any powers, neither height nor depth, nor anything else in all creation, will be able to separate us from the love of God that is in Christ Jesus our Lord.

"God made him who had no sin to be sin for us, so that in him we might become the righteousness of God" (2 Cor. 5:21). On the cross, God took our sins and placed them onto Jesus. Jesus's shedding of blood was the life given to us. Without the shedding of blood, there cannot be forgiveness. Jesus became sin, my sin. He bled on a cross so we don't have to be ashamed for the things we have done. Because of Jesus, we are the righteousness of Christ and no longer looked upon as a sinner. When God looks at us, He sees Jesus. Jesus is alive today and working in our lives in powerful ways if we will let Him. Will you take His hand?

"Therefore, if anyone is in Christ, the new creation has come: The old has gone, the new is here" (2 Cor. 5:17). This shedding of blood meant a whole new life is offered to us. Jesus is alive. His finished work on the cross releases the power to restore what the enemy has taken.

Jesus came to this earth to fulfill Isaiah 61. This was His personal charter, one of which He read in the synagogue as He began His ministry. Jesus offers a new beginning, a fresh start. When you accept Him as your personal Lord and Savior, your sins are tossed into the sea of forgetfulness, never to be brought up again. When Jesus died on the cross, His work created all things new for you. A garment of salvation and a robe of righteousness are placed on you. When God looks at you, He sees Jesus. Isaiah 61:10 says, "I delight greatly in the LORD; my soul rejoices in my God. For he has clothed me with garments of salvation and arrayed me in a robe of his righteousness, as a bridegroom adorns his head like a priest, and as a bride adorns herself with her jewels."

Have you ever had someone do something really great for you that changed your life? Did you feel joy? I want you to let it sink in what Jesus did for you personally on the cross. Because of His work on the cross and His shed blood, you can share and open up the painful wounds to Him, and His healing touch mends them. Because of this, you can have great joy. Jesus is alive! His finished work on the cross is for you. So right now, I want you to close your eyes and visualize the most beautiful dress that you can. For the guys, I want you to visualize, however your heart and mind imagines, as being dressed in your finest garment.

Now open your eyes, and get ready for an assignment. Sometime this week for homework, I want you to begin creating your very own personal garment of salvation, a robe of righteousness. You are to work on visualizing and making the truth of who you are real for you. I suggest designing a beautiful dress/garment. However, you choose what method works best for you. What works for one may not work for another. I do suggest that, whatever you decide, the result is something concrete that you can refer back to as a reminder of who you are. This is a symbol of who you are in Christ.

This will be a visual aid of who you are in Christ. Be as creative as you like. I suggest using fabric, glitter, ribbon, and sequins, and just have fun with it. For the guys, be open to the process and design however you feel comfortable. It is an amazing process. Imagine and create. Take your time and continue to work on this throughout the rest of the book. You will see why this is of such importance as we move along.

The purpose of this assignment is to have you begin to imagine who you are and to design a dress or a garment that you can keep as a reminder of who you are. It is a tangible project that will be a constant reminder so there is no doubt as the enemy may attempt to make you feel that this is not true. As with anything, it takes practice and time for this to become solid in your heart and to know beyond a shadow of a doubt that this is true. Over time, this project will be a visual reminder of this truth.

I believe this is a vital step of the healing process as you realize your identity in Christ. As discussed earlier, what causes us to not see ourselves this way? Abuse, sin, and things that are done to us that create lies from the enemy. When a person has been abused, this individual very often feels he or she is bad or damaged in some way. This is called shame. This person may believe that what was done to him or her defines who he or she is or even that it was his or her fault or he or she caused it in some way. This is not true.

You are robed in a robe of righteousness. Nothing changes this. Things that happen to you do not define you. Nothing changes this robe. This is the essence of who you are once you accept Jesus's finished work on the cross. His finished work on the cross is why you wear this robe. This exercise will lay the foundation for further healing.

What is shame? Why do we have it? Is there hope to heal it?

One of Satan's lies is shame. What is shame? Webster's Dictionary 1913 defines shame as "a painful sensation excited by a consciousness of guilt or impropriety, or of having done something which injures reputation, or of the exposure of that which nature or modesty prompts us to conceal. Reproach incurred or suffered; dishonor; ignominy; derision; contempt."

Shame and guilt are very different. Guilt is a God-given emotion that happens when we sin. We confess our sins and we are forgiven. Shame, however, says that we as a person are bad with no value. It says that we are damaged goods. There is no separation between the behavior/actions of the person and the person as an individual.

Shame may begin when another person's actions or words shame us. It might be through abuse, neglect, or constant shaming words spoken over and over. When consistent condemning words are spoken over another person, that person begins to accept and to believe that these words are true. The person does not separate the person from the behavior. When these messages are repeated often enough, whether through words or actions, they become internalized into a core identity that says, "I am bad." And so the internal dialogue goes, "I must be bad to deserve such terrible treatment, it must be my fault, or something about me caused it." This becomes the person's core identity.

The healing of shame begins when a person identifies and confesses the biblical truth about who God says he or she is: robed in righteousness; a child of God; no longer condemned because of Jesus's work on the cross; and set apart. And the list is as long as the truths in the Bible. In addition, replace all lies counter to these statements with God's truth. And again take the wounds to Jesus.

I mention the next point because those who are shamed often think that, when someone hurts him or her, it is his or her fault. Make this statement real in the heart of the shamed person, "I am a good person. It is not my fault when another person hurts me." If that person is you, make this real for you. Shamed people gravitate toward feeling responsible, even for their abuse, the wrong behavior of the person hurting them.

When we do not see ourselves as God sees us in this beautiful dress/garment (robe of righteousness) or if we sin or make a mistake, we think we are bad. Recall the shame. The dress/garment homework helps you to begin to process and make as your own the truth in God's Word. It helps to solidify the fact that, no matter what you do, God still sees you as good. Nothing ever changes the dress/garment! And if you have sinned in your situation, there is great news. When you confess your sins, He is faithful and just to forgive your trespasses. He tosses them in the sea of forgetfulness. And once confessed, that is where we must leave them, never to be brought up again.

You are robed in a beautiful dress/garment and are always this way. And nothing ever changes this, no matter what happens to you. These things are separate from you. If another person hurt you, the behavior is the fault of that person who hurt you. These actions are not caused by you and absolutely do not define you. They have no effect on you as a person other than the hurt. And God made a plan for that hurt to heal you as you share the wounds with Jesus. So no matter what happens or happened, you are still dressed in a beautiful dress or garment. As you accept who you are and that this robe of righteousness is who you are, you will begin to take steps toward that person.

What happens to you does not define you. (This is where the dress/garment has healing value.) You are righteous, pure, and spotless.

And as you get the dress or garment and begin the process of healing past wounds and hurts and replacing enemy lies with the truth, then this will move from head knowledge to heart knowledge. This will rid you of the shame you have inside of you. Remember that the abuse or wrong action toward you is what created your feeling that you are bad in the first place. Have you ever sensed the words "I'm bad" when you do something wrong or when someone does something mean to you?

In my own life, I experienced this shame-based feeling that I was a bad person. I could not separate the action from myself as a person. In my case, the issue was my divorce decision. Yes, divorce is a sin, but upon confessing it, I should have moved on. I could not move on. I couldn't separate the behavior from the person. I couldn't get that because of all the shame from my childhood. You see, I accepted the shame that did not belong to me. I had to realize who I am and that nothing I did or was done to me changes that.

The robe of righteousness/dress/garment is on you. It's not a matter of what you do. It is who you are! When you accept Jesus, the robe of righteousness is placed on you. It has nothing to do with external things or behavior. It is who you are. So as you work on designing these dresses/garments, I want you to remind yourself in various ways just who you are. For example, do such things as leaving yourself little reminders that say you are robed in a robe of righteousness. Nothing changes this fact. Pull out the characteristics in the Bible of what your identity in Christ is and then place them on note cards in different places to remind yourself. Whatever it takes, do it. As you repeat these truths to yourself, you will start accepting the dress/garment. It will become real for you.

As you are digesting who you are by creating these beautiful dresses and garments, my prayer is that the Holy Spirit will begin revealing areas of past hurt that need the healing touch of Jesus. I suggest journaling. Write down your thoughts and feelings on paper. You can even begin asking the Lord to reveal to you areas needing healing. We all do things to protect ourselves when we are hurt. In addition, what lies have you been believing about yourself? When we experience abuse, trauma, hurt, or betrayal, oftentimes the enemy fabricates a lie, and it becomes truth to us. A lie is deception, and it is not true. These falsehoods have a negative impact on our lives. And while I will continue spending some time in future chapters discussing the concept of lies and truth, this is not a magic formula. This is the work of the Holy Spirit revealing areas needing healing and about God's timing. This is not about striving. This is about a personal relationship with Jesus.

Jesus died on cross for you, and nothing changes who you are. Nothing. You did not cause things to happen to you. It is not something you did or did not do that caused the hurt. You are robed in righteousness. Jesus made you that way. Nothing can happen to you that changes who you are. God sees a robe of righteousness. He designed you this way. God designed you in His image. When bad things happen, they are separate from you. And they absolutely do not define who you are. When another person hurts you, it is his or her fault. It is his or her bad behavior, not yours. You are the righteousness of Christ. Begin to imagine yourself in the dress/garment. Will you close your eyes and imagine right now? So take your time with this dress/garment exercise, and work on it throughout your journey. Really let this point sink in.

As we move forward in the journey, you will begin replacing the enemy lies with the truth of God. As you allow Jesus access to your heart by sharing your pain, His healing light will heal the wounds. Then the dress/garment is further solidified for you. You will finally get it and believe it from your heart, not just your head. Again this is a work of the Holy Spirit as He reveals these lies to you. This is about a personal relationship with the Lord. It is a process as you surrender to His leading. The power is released again through the work of Jesus on the cross.

My prayer through this process is that you will believe in your heart who you are in Christ. So have fun with this art project. Get out the glitter, the sequins, the ribbons, or whatever you decide to use to make this real for you. You also can begin to journal. And who knows? Maybe the Holy Spirit will reveal an area needing healing to you. You might even realize the lie you have been believing. Don't rush any of this. Take your time. This is a journey and not a race.

So be in prayer this week, asking God to reveal to you through the Holy Spirit any lies you have been believing. Use your journal in this process. And as always, share these wounds with Jesus opening up the wound. Give the pain to Jesus and allow the work of the cross, the power of the blood, to bring healing. As you do this, you will begin reclaiming your crown of beauty. Please realize, however, that healing is a lifelong process. You may revisit this throughout your lifetime in differing degrees for various wounds.

"Shout for joy, you heavens; rejoice, you earth; burst into song, you mountains! For the LORD comforts his people and will have compassion on his afflicted ones" (Isa. 49:13). To summarize, this is a process of getting head knowledge to heart knowledge, really getting it. When you get it that who you are in Christ does not change when things are done to you, that these things do not stick to you, there is joy. As you recognize any lies that you have been believing, you will begin the process of replacing these falsehoods with truth. As you allow Jesus to heal the wounds, then the dress/garment is further solidified for you. You will finally get it and believe it from your heart, not just your head.

You can tell a person over and over who he or she is and that unacceptable things that happen to him or her do not define him or her. But he or she will never get it until the head knowledge moves to the heart. My prayer for you is that you will truly realize who you are!

Isaiah 61:7–11 says,

> Instead of your shame you will receive a double portion, and instead of disgrace you will rejoice in your inheritance. And so you will inherit a double portion in your land, and everlasting joy will be yours. "For I, the LORD, love justice; I hate robbery and wrongdoing. In my faithfulness I will reward my people and make an everlasting covenant with them." Their descendants will be known among the nations and their offspring among the peoples. All who see them will acknowledge that they are a people the LORD has blessed. I delight greatly in the LORD; my soul rejoices in my God. For he has clothed me with garments of salvation and arrayed me in a robe of his righteousness, as a bridegroom adorns his head like a priest, and as a bride adorns herself with her jewels. For as the soil makes the sprout come up and a garden causes seeds to grow, so the Sovereign LORD will make righteousness and praise spring up before all nations.

CHAPTER 7

If Only I Believed

I love the ocean. Have you ever stood beside the ocean until you were lost in its magnificence? God's unfailing love for you is deeper, wider, and more powerful than any ocean. Not only that, God wants to redeem you. This is why He sent His Son Jesus to restore all that the enemy has taken from you. My prayer is that, as you read this book, you will receive a revelation (believe and know) of who you are in Christ and, from this point, walk in restoration and freedom.

What is it about a contrast that gets our attention? In the movies, there is usually a plot of evil and good. In the restaurant industry, there is always a five star and a one star. In the new car industry, there is the JD Power automotive ratings. In the hotel industry, it is no different. Each sector has a rating system where we go to make the perfect buyer's choice. On top of that, awards are given for the best whatever.

In a world filled with making the best buying choice and having the best whatever, there is one thing that is rated the highest rating ever achieved—you. Because of Jesus and the cross, no matter what, you are perfect and set apart. And if you want to research and back that up with facts, please go to the Holy Bible.

Who You Are in Christ

"Therefore, there is now no condemnation for those who are in Christ Jesus" (Rom. 8:1). And Romans 8:31–39 says,

What, then, shall we say in response to these things? If God is for us, who can be against us? He who did not spare his own Son, but gave him up for us all—how will he not also, along with him, graciously give us all things? Who will bring any charge against those whom God has chosen? It is God who justifies. Who then is the one who condemns? No one. Christ Jesus who died—more than that, who was raised to life—is at the right hand of God and is also interceding for us. Who shall separate us from the love of Christ? Shall trouble or hardship or persecution or famine or nakedness or danger or sword? As it is written: "For your sake we face death all day long; we are considered as sheep to be slaughtered." No, in all these things we are more than conquerors through him who loved us. For I am convinced that neither death nor life, neither angels nor demons, neither the present nor the future, nor any powers, neither height nor depth, nor anything else in all creation, will be able to separate us from the love of God that is in Christ Jesus our Lord.

"God made him who had no sin to be sin for us, so that in him we might become the righteousness of God" (2 Cor. 5:21).

On the cross, God took all the sins of the world and placed them onto Jesus. Can you even fathom the love that God has for you that He would do this to His only Son? Jesus's shedding of blood was the life given to us. The power of the cross transforms lives. Jesus came to redeem and to restore, to give back all that has been taken in life's journey. Because of His shed blood and work on the cross, we can find healing. Jesus is alive today, and He is our only source of hope. Without the shedding of blood, there cannot be forgiveness. Jesus became sin, my sin. He bled on a cross so we don't have to be ashamed for what we have done. Because of Jesus, we become the righteousness of Christ. When God looks at us, He sees Jesus. When Jesus died on the cross, His shed blood created all things new for you. A garment of salvation and a robe of righteousness was placed on you.

What makes us not see ourselves this way? I will continue the discussion from the last chapter. The unacceptable things that happen to us and around us. In addition, to this, things that we ourselves might have done. However, things that happen to you do not define you. Things that you have done do not define you. Nothing changes this robe. You are righteous, pure and beautiful. This is the essence of who you are once you accept Jesus's finished work on the cross. No matter what is done to us or what we do, nothing changes this robe of righteousness.

Let's say you find yourself homeless. You begin to wonder: how did I get to this point? You replay over and over how this might have happened. You are caught in a tailspin and downward cycle of self-blame and self-loathing.

Let me stop you there. Life is difficult, and it's not about how you got here. It is all about who you are and what has been done for you! When Jesus was crucified, He was first nailed to the cross while it lay on the ground, and then the soldiers lifted the cross with Him on it high. Just as Jesus was lifted higher on the cross, when you are down, because of what Jesus did for you, He lifts you higher. You rise above the circumstances of life.

And so I ask you: have you ever reached a tipping point? Well, one day I had enough. I was filled with fear and the realization that I had absolutely no control of my life. I finally confessed this to God and fully surrendered this fear. It was as if there were a shift in the atmosphere. At this point, God began giving me wisdom about the underlying lies that I was believing and on and on. I share this because surrender is the essential ingredient to opening ourselves up to the healing work of the cross.

"For to us a child is born, to us a son is given, and the government will be on his shoulders. And he will be called Wonderful Counselor, Mighty God, Everlasting Father, Prince of Peace" (Isa. 9:6).

For me, when I experienced my painful experience of the death of my mother, I found myself angry with God. Although I knew who

He was and recognized that He loved me, when I prayed, I began not looking at Him directly. I am not sure why, but often God gets the brunt of our anger when we are hurt. For me, I began to think things like, "Because God is sovereign, He could have stopped this, but He did not."

This is human nature, but God is always good, and He does not take pleasure when the enemy hurts us. We need to start putting the blame where it belongs, on the enemy. God promises in Romans 8:28 that all things work together to those who love the Lord. God is the one with the restoration plan, the one who will turn it all around and heal our hurts.

Jesus came to redeem and to restore, to give back all that has been taken in life's journey. Jesus is alive today, and He is your only source of hope. Jesus came "to proclaim freedom for the captives and release from darkness for the prisoners" (Isa. 61:1).

Through my personal journey and a revelation of God's healing power, He revealed the key to receiving the truth of who we are in Christ. It is my sincere desire that the reality of who you are in Christ will settle into your heart.

For illustration sake, I want to make a point with a comparison of how we can hear lies from the enemy, with truth as the contrast.

Lies	*Truth*
shattered	restored
hopeless	joyful
worthless	significant
damaged	perfect

When I consider this, it brings one question to mind: Is it possible to truly believe in my heart the truth about me? In the last chapter, I gave you a homework assignment. You were asked to work on visualizing that you wear a robe of righteousness and to begin making the truth of who you are real for you. God's truth is for both female and male, all people. I suggested designing a beautiful dress/garment. You choose what method works best for you. What works for one may not work for another. I do recommend that, whatever you decide, the result is something concrete that you can refer back to as a reminder of who you are. This is a symbol of who you are in Christ.

But may I ask you one question: at this moment, do you believe this is true in your heart? "The heart is deceitful above all things and beyond cure. Who can understand it" (Jer. 17:9). I'm challenging you today to make this real for you. That is to move this truth to your heart. If you do, it will change your life. We are going to take some time to discuss this very concept.

Henry David Thoreau once said, "As a single footstep will not make a path on the earth, so a single thought will not make a pathway in the mind. To make a deep physical path, we walk again and again. To make a deep mental path, we must think over and over the kind of thoughts we wish to dominate our lives."

Once again, I want to speak again to the dress/garment and who you are in Christ, but also touch on some things that can hinder your belief that this is true for you. You can tell a person the truth over and over again that the unacceptable things that happened to him or her is not his or her fault, but it won't work unless this individual believes it. And I will expand on that. You can tell a person the truth over and over again that the things that happen to him or her are not a part of who he or she is. It won't work unless this person believes it. Therefore, what we are working toward is having you believe this from your heart. We are using a visual concept to make this happen.

Are you beginning to process and think about what your dress/garment might look like? As you spend time designing a beautiful dress/garment, allow this to serve as a symbol of the truth about you. The truth, as spoken by God, is in the scripture Isaiah 61:10. Will you read that with me again right now? What does this truth mean to you? "I delight greatly in the LORD; my soul rejoices in my God. For he has clothed me with garments of salvation and arrayed me in a robe of his righteousness, as a bridegroom adorns his head like a priest, and as a bride adorns herself with her jewels" (Isa. 61:10).

This scripture is truth about you. This is the essence of who you are in Christ. This means, if you have accepted Christ as your Savior and Lord, this promise is for you.

Let's talk about how the truth and believing is important. Even when we know in our head that we are dressed this way, it may not be in our heart. So we will go further. We will discuss in-depth the concepts of lies, truth, the healing of past wounds, and the replacing of falsehoods with truth. And we will discuss how these will seal the truth about you.

Let's return to the challenge. Do you believe the following: that you wear a robe of righteousness, that God sees Jesus when He looks at you, that you are righteous and pure, and that you are not a bad person, somehow damaged or unfit to wear this robe? Or are you believing lies from the enemy? Do you believe that you wear a robe of righteousness/garment of salvation? Do you believe that there is no condemnation for you? Or do you believe the condemning lies of the enemy?

If you don't, let me ask you a question. What is stopping you from seeing yourself this way? Could it be that the fallen world that we live in—with all of its abuse, sin, and things that happen to us—has created lies and deception from the enemy that have impacted you and caused your doubt? Again you are robed in a robe of righteousness. Nothing changes this. Things that happen to you do not define you. Nothing changes this robe. You are pure and beautiful. This is the essence of who you are once you accept Jesus's finished work on the cross. Remember that His finished work on the cross is why you wear this robe. Begin to imagine yourself in the dress/garment. Will you close your eyes and envision right now?

Will you choose to believe and accept Jesus and what He did for you on the cross? Will you make the choice to believe? And if you struggle with belief, ask God to help you. God promises to help you with any unbelief. You are worth more than diamonds. You are priceless. The truth is found in the pages of the Bible. The lies are found in the world; the lies are from the enemy.

We can create a thousand dresses and walk around saying, "I am wearing a garment of salvation. I am robed in righteousness." But if we do not believe it from our heart, it changes nothing. We still walk around defeated. Until the veil of unbelief is removed, these are empty words.

The Bible says, "The god of this age has blinded the minds of unbelievers, so that they cannot see the light of the gospel that displays the glory of Christ, who is the image of God" (2 Cor. 4:4).

What is the meaning of believe? Webster's Dictionary 1913 defines believe as "to have a firm persuasion, esp. of the truths of religion; to have a persuasion approaching to certainty; to exercise belief or faith."

This is a process of moving head knowledge to heart knowledge, really getting it. The healing comes from the process of realizing who you are in Christ (the dress/garment and nothing that happens to us defines us) + the Holy Spirit revealing any lies you may have made when you were hurt + the enemy lies being replaced with the truth (God's truth)

And ultimately sharing all of the pain and opening your wounds to the healing power of the blood of Jesus brings healing to your wounds. Then the dress/garment/visual aid is further solidified for you. You will finally get it and believe it from your heart, not just your head.

Let's look at my list for a moment. What would happen if I really believed this about myself?

Lies	Truth
shattered	restored
hopeless	joyful
worthless	significant
damaged	perfect

Isaiah 61:1 says, "To proclaim freedom for the captives and release from darkness for the prisoners." In order for this to happen, we must allow Jesus full access to our innermost heart. We must surrender. We must share our personal pain, all of it, and allow the healing light of

Jesus to touch it. The starting point is first believing in Jesus as our Lord and Savior and then onto believing the truths found in God's Word, that you are who Isaiah 61:10 says you are. We can make a thousand dresses, but until we believe that we are robed in righteousness, it has no meaning.

Hope is very much a part of this process. For you see, if we do not have the hope that Jesus Christ gave us on the cross, then we have no hope of healing from our pain, both past and present. I grew up in an environment where unacceptable things were happening, where I never knew what might happen. As a child, I daydreamed about the day when all of the pain would go away. Can you imagine the pain I must have felt? Well, one thing I always looked forward to was the day I graduated high school. Things would be different. For you see, I had a seed of hope within me that was planted at an early age. If things are difficult for you right now, there is hope that things will not always be this way.

During my journey, I received countless sequins of hope. I recognized how God heals from past abuse and wounds and how recognizing the dress and who I am in Christ was so important. As the Holy Spirit led, I began recognizing lies and deceit from the enemy, who always seeks to destroy, and from that, I began replacing these falsehoods with truth (God's truth).

This is a work of the Holy Spirit as He reveals these lies to us. I learned that, when I opened up my heart and shared the pain, allowing the healing light of Jesus to touch it, I found healing. This was only because of the work of the cross, the power of the blood, that brings healing. Remember that healing is a process and sometimes occurs over a lifetime as God reveals areas that need healing. Again, this is not an overnight, immediate thing. It is a process as we surrender to His leading. The power is because of the work of Jesus on the cross.

An Unexpected Healing

How many of us walk around with unhealed memories from our childhood? It might be memories of a particular event or perhaps a history of a dysfunctional childhood. I can imagine most people can think of something. However, many times, we carry around unhealed emotions and we do not even remember the full details of what may have happened during that time. For me, the Lord began revealing to me details of my childhood which brought unexpected healing to me.

We have talked about journaling, and I highly recommend it. Please remember that the Holy Spirit is your helper and will guide you in the process. The first step is to write out everything you can recall. Once complete, take the words you wrote to the Lord and share the thoughts and feelings, all of it. As you begin to share all that you recall of the painful event, the Holy Spirit will reveal lies, and the truth will come during this process.

Once the lie is exposed, you take the lie and allow the Holy Spirit to share what the thought process was that served as fuel to the falsehood. Again, journaling helps. This lie is then replaced with facts that are true, God's truth and what His Word says. Ultimately the sharing of these wounds and all of the pain with Jesus and allowing His light to touch those wounds brings healing.

In addition, the Lord may take you back in time. For example, the Lord took me back in my memory, and I could literally smell the house I grew up in. And as I cried and felt the pain as if I were a little girl, Jesus healed my heart, and I, in turn, expressed my anger and hurt. I shared everything I was thinking and feeling. I held nothing back. And you know what? I was healed.

Who was present with me that day in my healing of these past wounds? Jesus, myself, and my journal. Please note that the Holy Spirit will reveal to you the specifics of your healing so you don't have to strive to figure things out. Surrender and rest in the Holy Spirit's leading in both timing and healing.

This is a process of getting head knowledge to heart knowledge, really getting it. When you get it that who you are in Christ does not change when things are done to you, and that these things do not stick to you, there is joy. As you recognize any lies that you have been believing, you will begin the process of replacing these falsehoods with truth. As you open up your wounds and allow Jesus to heal them, then the dress/garment is further solidified for you. You will finally get it and believe it from your heart, not just your head.

As I have shared this concept with others in the past, I am amazed at the results. And, as you work, it may take you time to process this assignment, and at first, you may not be sure where to begin. That is just fine. I suggest that you continue reading the book in order to digest more messages and words of hope about who you are in Christ. And as you do, all of the sequins, fabric, glitter, and everything else will become building blocks to create your own personal dress/garment. Your dress/garment will be spectacular, and each one will have personal attributes on them. When you work with open hearts, the results will be stunning.

"He predestined us for adoption to sonship through Jesus Christ, in accordance with his pleasure and will" (Eph. 1:5).

CHAPTER 8

Beauty from Ashes

"'I have seen their ways, but I will heal them; I will guide them and restore comfort to Israel's mourners, creating praise on their lips. Peace, peace, to those far and near,' says the LORD. 'And I will heal them'" (Isa. 57:18–19).

Have you ever felt like everything in your life seems dead or hopeless? Have you felt that your dreams, your hopes, and your life has come to a stop? In Ezekiel 37, the prophet Ezekiel had a vision. He saw a valley of dead bones coming to life right in front of him. "This is what the Sovereign LORD says to these bones: I will make breath enter you, and you will come to life" (Ezek. 37:5).

How can dead bones possibly come to life? With God, all things are possible. In this chapter, Ezekiel was describing restoration to new life as well as a future time when there would be restoration for Israel. God is all about restoration, and just like this prophetic vision, God will exchange beauty for the ashes in our lives. For you see, restoration is synonymous with (new) life.

When I lost my mom, I felt this way. I felt like everything had died with her. She was my rock, my cheerleader, my protector. She was not just my mom but my best friend. She was my light, and when she died, my world seemed dark and empty. But guess what? God had a restoration plan all prepared for me.

My sister Cara and brother-in-law Bill came alongside me and filled the empty spaces in my life. They journeyed with me and offered me hope. I was angry with God during this time so I did not reach out immediately to Him, but they led me back to the Lord. Though I may have not recognized that was happening at the time, they were planting sequins of hope. They comforted me with hope.

"Praise be to the God and Father of our Lord Jesus Christ, the Father of compassion and the God of all comfort, who comforts us in all our troubles, so that we can comfort those in any trouble with the comfort we ourselves receive from God" (2 Cor. 1:3–4).

It is my prayer that the words on these pages may in some way comfort you and give you hope. During my dark time, hope came for me in the form of a new employee at my job. This person shared a book with me by Max Lucado called *He Still Moves Stones*. A scripture jumped off one of the pages of that book and brought me back to the Lord. The scripture was, "A bruised reed he will not break, and a smoldering wick he will not snuff out" (Isa. 42:3). For me, part of my anger at God was that I felt that He caused my brokenness and that He did not care. This was a lie. This was the truth I needed to get me back on the path.

Today as I write these words, I just now realize why that scripture changed me that day. You see, God has a restoration plan for you, and sometimes that plan might look like a person or even as a book. And while I may not have realized just why that scripture had changed me, it does not take away from the reality that it did. God is sovereign over all matters, and He knew what it would take to get my attention. Why would He do this if He doesn't care? You see, that was a lie from the enemy. God does care. He breathes life and hope into the hopeless situations.

"This is what God the LORD says—the Creator of the heavens, who stretches them out, who spreads out the earth with all that springs from it, who gives breath to its people, and life to those who walk on it" (Isa. 42:5).

When trauma or crises hit, we often look around, and everything seems destroyed, like a desert without hope. As we sit in the shock and the ashes, Jesus weeps with us. Because of Jesus, we have hope, and He holds out His hand to pick us up from the ashes. One day there will be full restoration, and all things will become like Eden, as Isaiah 35 so beautifully describes. But also today, because of the power of the cross, we are promised hope and restoration, that is, new life. So let's take Jesus's hand and continue on our journey. Today we are walking on the beach, and as we trod along, I believe I can see those silver sparkles in the sand. Can you?

This is a journey to new life. As we view the perspective of new life, we see the image of a flower bud opening. The Lord gave me this image as we were considering and praying about a possible big family decision. I saw the vision of a flower opening up, and at once, I knew we were on the right track. God is a God of restoration, and as quickly as we face darkness and pain, the Lord is already planning how He will restore and redeem all that the enemy came to take.

You know, often it is in retrospect that we realize how our faith has been built in the journey. Tonight I decided to do some rearranging at home. As I place my perfect conch shell that is ten inches in diameter on the table, I think about how God always does and gives us more than we can ask or imagine. On that particular part of my journey, I received a blessing, a vacation with an excursion to Grand Turk Island. As I was walking on the beach that afternoon, I asked the Lord for a seashell. In my mind, I imagined a perfect shell perhaps an inch or two in diameter, something I could treasure in my heart.

As I walked on the shore, I saw something in the water. I reached down to get it and literally fell to my knees. I asked Mark if he would go pick up the light colored object in the water. He reached in and picked up a gorgeous peach and terra cotta colored conk shell. It was huge and absolutely stunning. I was reminded of the fact that God always gives us amazingly more than we can ever ask for. And as I write this, I realize that what has brought you to your knees may be the very thing that leads God to give you more than you could ever imagine or ask for. God loves you, and He is a good and perfect Father. His character never changes despite the troubles we encounter.

I once heard the phrase, "A healing comes from a wounding." Though it sounds logical in the physical sense, we cut our finger. It heals. No biggie, huh? What I am talking about here is a healing of our heart, something much deeper. Because of Jesus's death on the cross and His wounding, we receive the power of the blood on the cross, healing for the wounds in our lives. God wants to take the brokenness of our lives and turn it into something beautiful. "And provide for those who grieve in Zion—to bestow on them a crown of beauty instead of ashes, the oil of joy instead of mourning, and a garment of praise instead of a spirit of despair. They will be called oaks of righteousness, a planting of the LORD for the display of his splendor" (Isa. 61:3).

In the days of the Old Testament, when people were in mourning, they put on sackcloth and ashes, a symbol of mourning. Can you imagine in the midst of a horrible situation that you would put these ashes on your head or that you would just sit in a pile of ashes? Can you imagine the level of hopelessness that would cause you to do this? On the contrary, God is saying He is going to lift you from the ashes and give you beauty. Have you ever had a situation where you were in the darkest, most difficult trial of your life? Maybe it is right now? So God does care, and He is concerned about you and your situation. To give you beauty for ashes?

"Why me?" you ask.

God loves you as a daughter or son. He is your Father, better than any earthly father. You are His prized daughter or son. You are a daughter or son of the King. In the book of Isaiah, it says, "To proclaim the year of the LORD's favor and the day of vengeance of our God, to comfort all who mourn" (Isa. 61:2). God is our comforter. He wants to comfort, heal, redeem, and restore you. He realizes that bad things can and do happen to us. God knew that life would bring hurt, trauma, and devastation, but He promises to turn the ashes into something beautiful, if we will allow Him.

"In all their distress he too was distressed, and the angel of his presence saved them. In his love and mercy he redeemed them; he lifted them up and carried them all the days of old" (Isa. 63:9). God is a loving, compassionate God who cares about your situation. I have received many reminders of His plan to restore and just as many of His plans to deliver and save. He is mighty to save! Will you cry out to him?

God sometimes uses the most horrible of situations to heal us, to make us stronger and more like Christ. Sometimes the only way we will heal is to be broken. Occasionally it is the only way that we will surrender to His purpose and plan. I am speaking to myself now. I had a lot of pride that the Lord had to remove. God can take the very darkest of circumstances and turn them into a launching pad toward a new beginning.

Here is how this might look. It can happen in a myriad of ways. God can use anything to heal you. Something happens. It might be trauma, crises, loss, or betrayal, essentially a hurt. I describe it as a defining moment. Something happens that changes the way you previously saw life. Like me, it might be from the past, for example, your childhood. At these moments, we begin to carry this thing that stays with us, and we don't even realize it. It can be there for years until something or the Holy Spirit brings it to the surface. Healing is a lifetime experience and a process.

How many of you learn better by examples? I am one of those people who learn better this way. I love illustrations. So later in this chapter. I will share with you some examples of how this looked in my journey.

"Shout for joy, you heavens; rejoice, you earth; burst into song, you mountains! For the LORD comforts his people and will have compassion on his afflicted ones" (Isa. 49:13). God wants to take your broken places, those hurts as spoken of in Isaiah 61:3, and heal them. He desires to bring beauty from ashes. Are you willing to surrender and allow God to exchange your ashes for beauty? You only need to release the hurts to Jesus and allow Him to shine His healing light on these wounds.

> To the Jews who had believed him, Jesus said, "If you
> hold to my teaching, you are really my disciples. Then
> you will know the truth, and the truth will set you free."
> They answered him, "We are Abraham's descendants
> and have never been slaves of anyone. How can you say
> that we shall be set free?" Jesus replied, "Very truly I tell
> you, everyone who sins is a slave to sin. Now a slave has
> no permanent place in the family, but a son belongs to

it forever. So if the Son sets you free, you will be free indeed" (John 8:31–36).

Jesus is still today holding out His hand for all who will come to Him, realizing He is the one Messiah, the Savior, and the Son of God. So pick up your journal as you walk your journey to new life. And remember this is about the journey, not a destination. Jesus will heal as you are ready to open up your heart and in His timing. This is not about striving. If anything, it is the opposite. Whenever I found myself striving, that is, working from my own thoughts or strength, I found I had lost a sequin of hope. This is about surrendering, for in my times of surrendering, the Lord showed up in amazing ways. This is about a personal relationship with the Lord and a surrendered heart.

Ralph Waldo Emerson once said, "We become what we think about all day long."

The dresses/garments or other visual you made are a reminder and symbol of who you are and a reflection of your identity in Christ. I pray that you will frame these dresses/garments and keep them as a reminder of this truth.

As you may recall, I had mentioned in a previous chapter that the Holy Spirit is our counselor. "But when he, the Spirit of truth, comes, he will guide you into all the truth. He will not speak on his own; he will speak only what he hears, and he will tell you what is yet to come" (John 16:13). This was Jesus announcing the promise of the Holy Spirit. Because of Jesus's shed blood and His work on the cross, once we accept Jesus into our heart, we are sealed with the Holy Spirit, which will guide us into all truth. The Holy Spirit will reveal to you what you do not know to heal.

"You belong to your father, the devil, and you want to carry out your father's desires. He was a murderer from the beginning, not holding to the truth, for there is no truth in him. When he lies, he speaks his native language, for he is a liar and the father of lies" (John 8:44).

Satan works to make us believe lies about ourselves and others. One year at Halloween, we attended an outreach event in our community. It was a hope house rather than a haunted house. In it were various rooms and scenes from the lives of different people who were struggling with life issues. In one of the scenes was a character dressed like the enemy. And guess what he was doing? He was literally whispering lies into the ear of these individuals. One was a young girl who cut herself. The enemy was taunting her and telling her lies. The enemy was telling her to cut herself and saying that she was worthless. This is how the enemy works. My prayer is that you will recognize these lies and replace them with God's truth. The enemy speaks falsehoods to ruin our lives and to destroy us.

I am reminded of that day when we found a wounded butterfly. As it lay on the sand, I could see it gasp, almost as if it were taking its last breath. We picked it up and carried it to an area providing shelter from the wind. As it lay there, we began to speak words of hope and life to it. It started as a game, and then we soon realized that it seemed like our words were giving life to the butterfly. It soon began to flap its wings. This was an incredible gift from the Lord because we saw a visual of how God's truth spoken over our lives brings healing to our wounds. It was as if we were speaking life into this little butterfly. I am reminded of how God breathes life into us.

How many of you learn better through the use of examples? I am going to share with you two examples of times when the Lord revealed to me that it was time to heal, that it was time to bring this pain to Jesus. The first was a "jot down" moment; the second was a trigger. I call this a jot down moment, because we may often become aware of something important in the healing process at an unexpected time. That is, we want to write it down and return to it at a time when we can journal it and bring it before the Lord. These are but two of the ways that the Holy Spirit may reveal areas needing healing. A lie might be exposed simply from thinking something about yourself that is contrary to what God's Word says you are. Or it might come from a strong overreaction to something that might not normally warrant such a reaction. As you can see, there are a myriad of different ways as distinct as each unique individual.

Example #1

It was a Saturday afternoon, and I began sharing with Mark about a particular afternoon from my childhood. Before I share this story, I want to say that I would not trade my childhood because it made me the person that I am today. The Lord revealed to me that my dad had suffered abuse in his life and through my journey of understanding this, I was able to understand him which brought both forgiveness and healing to me. Anyhow, on with the story. I had just gotten home after school, and I was eating dinner. My dad always picked on me when I got off the bus after school. I remember not wanting to get off the bus in the afternoon. This particular day, I'd had enough. I was sitting and eating my dinner when my dad just kept picking on me. Something came over me, and I threw my food across the room at him. And then before I knew it, we were arguing.

I told him that day, "Do not pick on me like this again."

After I said this, I remembered feeling very guilty. I recalled confessing this sin to the Lord when it happened.

Mark's first words were, "You are still very angry."

I was shocked, but those five words were accurate. I had not healed from that day.

Mark said, "That was a defining moment for you. You weren't going to let him do that to you anymore."

It was a defining moment in my life, and what happened on this particular Saturday is what I call a "jot down" moment. The Holy Spirit had brought this to my attention. Upon realizing that I was still angry about that day, I did something different this time. I began to journal what happened that day. I have learned that, when you have a moment like this, it helps to get your thoughts on paper.

The Lord began to show me that this process is much deeper than just writing words on a paper. It was deeper because these thoughts and feelings must be shared in prayer with Jesus to allow His healing touch on the open wounds, which brings healing. So I began writing every detail.

Once finished, I went back and prayed what I had written and asked the Lord to mend my wounds. It is very therapeutic to take our hurts before the Lord and allow His healing light to touch them. I had never experienced the power of Jesus's work on the cross until that day.

As I began to process what I had written in my journal, that is, what I was sharing with the Lord, God took me back to how I felt. It was almost if I could see and smell that house. I began to express how I felt as a little girl and how angry I was at my dad. I realized I decided a few things that day. First, I was very hurt, and no one would ever treat me this way again. Without realizing it then, I began believing a lie that day that I had to protect myself. This led to a wall, which I was not aware of, self-protection. In my relationships, I had built a wall.

So you see, it was a twofold process of healing. First, I had a "jot down" moment. I recognized that I should not be still angry and began to question why I was still fuming after all of these years about that one day. Second, I took it before the Lord (as journaling does help) and asked Him why I was feeling this way.

God revealed to me that I had made a promise to myself that day that "no one would ever treat me that way ever again." In my heart, I categorized all people as being this way, the lie. The falsehood took root when my dad hurt me that day. I began believing the lie that all people are like my dad so I must protect myself and certainly not allow this type of behavior toward me.

As I recognized this wound, I took it and shared it with Jesus. I allowed His healing light to touch my wounds. I cried, and I felt angry over what happened that day. I even pretended my dad was sitting in a chair as I told him how I felt. Then I came to a point where I pitied my dad and was able to forgive him for that day. I realized that I had formed an opinion of my dad that was not correct. His behavior most likely came from hurt he had experienced in his life. What came out of this? I became softer as my protective wall came down. I began extending more grace toward others when they crossed me. It was transforming for my relationships. This is another example of the healing power of Jesus.

Example #2

In the second example, I was experiencing a trigger, which is when a current situation subconsciously reminds you of a past event (unhealed) so you overreact to the current situation. I was finding myself overreacting every time there was chaos in my house.

How many of you know that there will be chaos at times in your house especially if you have several people living in the house? I realized that I should not be overreacting like this, so I prayed and asked the Holy Spirit to reveal to me why I was acting this way. God revealed why this was happening, I shared these wounds with Jesus, and I was able to heal. "The heart is deceitful above all things and beyond cure. Who can understand it?" (Jer. 17:9).

Pray for God's truth to be revealed to you about what you remember if you are dealing with something in the past. While God may not reveal every single detail, He will reveal what you need to heal. Remember this is not about striving. God's truth about your bondage can lead to restoration. I'm a testimony that this is real. Notice that I asked the tough questions and the Holy Spirit answered and revealed me things I would not have known. God is a God of restoration, and He healed my broken emotions. He will do the same for you.

"For the word of God is living and active and sharper than any two-edged sword, and piercing as far as the division of soul and spirit, of both joints and marrow, and able to judge the thoughts and intentions of the heart" (Heb. 4:12).

And so this is a journey to new life. As you can see, part of the journey is when we recover from things we thought we had forgotten long ago in our past. The Lord is so loving and filled with grace that out of our current pain and heartache can also come mending from wounds long ago. Just as Jesus was wounded and brought us healing, so too we can be wounded and find His healing.

Have you ever watched the excitement of a child finding a caterpillar? When my daughter was little, she found a prized one at my sister Cara's house. She placed it in her screened container along with water and leaves for food. She was so excited. That night after she had gone to bed,

Cara and I noticed that the caterpillar was very lethargic, and it looked like it had died. So we devised a grand scheme to find another caterpillar and put it in the cage so the next day she could experience the same joy she had that day. Well, guess what? This particular caterpillar wasn't as stunning looking, and she soon noticed our little scheme.

You know what? I later realized that we had tossed out the caterpillar when it was preparing to cocoon itself. Why? We wanted the beauty right there in the moment. In time, this lethargic caterpillar would have become a beautiful butterfly. We missed the beauty of new life and a butterfly because we threw in the towel and tossed the caterpillar. We felt that having it lying there wasn't providing enjoyment for her. We tossed out the hope!

Just like that caterpillar who would have morphed into a beautiful butterfly had we given it time, new life and restoration is a process. We have to be patient as God does His work. Don't toss out your hope! Don't throw away your caterpillar because beauty from ashes and life from dead bones is promised and it is right around the corner. "Since ancient times no one has heard, no ear has perceived, no eye has seen any God besides you, who acts on behalf of those who wait for him" (Isa. 64:4). We have no idea how God will act on our behalf. When we wait for Him in faith, we confidently expect that He will act. I know how difficult this can be, but hold on. Your miracle just might be your next step.

And, so I wonder where you are today in your journey. My prayer is that you are experiencing hope and healing. And, that you are imagining yourself in your dress/garment. I can imagine Jesus placing a crown upon your head.

Are you like I was wounded by the word curses that had been spoken over you? God wants to restore you to the son/daughter that you are. My prayer is that you will also find that joy, and the crown of beauty will be restored to you.

"To all who mourn in Israel, he will give a crown of beauty for ashes, a joyous blessing instead of mourning, festive praise instead of despair. In their righteousness, they will be like great oaks that the LORD has planted for his own glory" (Isa. 61:3 NLT).

CHAPTER 9

A White Flag Called Victory

It was a day that began with everything at stake. It was an impossible situation. An important meeting would happen that day that would determine a series of events that would change everything. The chips were down in most areas, and it appeared that we were about to face our own personal Goliath. We were up against an impossible situation.

Have you ever felt this way? Have you ever felt like you are on the short end of the stick? That you have done everything that you thought was right and now it appears that you are on the road to ruin, be that financial, personal, or professional?

Recently my family and I spent a weekend in the mountains at a resort, a place known for its spa, a site full of the blessings of rejuvenation and known for its healing waters. Today I am asking you to journey with me up another mountain, one where you will receive a blessing. But not just any mountain. I want you to journey to Mount Moriah. As we travel, we see an older gentleman walking beside his son. The son is carrying something, wood. What strikes me as we go is the confidence in this man's steps. This man appears to have his mind set on where he is going. He is looking straight ahead.

> Then God said, "Take your son, your only son, whom
> you love—Isaac—and go to the region of Moriah.
> Sacrifice him there as a burnt offering on a mountain I
> will show you." Early the next morning Abraham got

up and loaded his donkey. He took with him two of his servants and his son Isaac. When he had cut enough wood for the burnt offering, he set out for the place God had told him about. On the third day Abraham looked up and saw the place in the distance. He said to his servants, "Stay here with the donkey while I and the boy go over there. We will worship and then we will come back to you." Abraham took the wood for the burnt offering and placed it on his son Isaac, and he himself carried the fire and the knife. As the two of them went on together, Isaac spoke up and said to his father Abraham, "Father?" "Yes, my son?" Abraham replied. "The fire and wood are here," Isaac said, "but where is the lamb for the burnt offering?" Abraham answered, "God himself will provide the lamb for the burnt offering, my son." And the two of them went on together. When they reached the place God had told him about, Abraham built an altar there and arranged the wood on it. He bound his son Isaac and laid him on the altar, on top of the wood. Then he reached out his hand and took the knife to slay his son. But the angel of the LORD called out to him from heaven, "Abraham! Abraham!" "Here I am," he replied. "Do not lay a hand on the boy," he said. "Do not do anything to him. Now I know that you fear God, because you have not withheld from me your son, your only son." Abraham looked up and there in a thicket he saw a ram caught by its horns. He went over and took the ram and sacrificed it as a burnt offering instead of his son. So Abraham called that place The LORD Will Provide. And to this day it is said, "On the mountain of the LORD it will be provided" (Gen. 22:1–14).

Wow! What strikes me about this is Abraham's unbridled choice to obey God, despite what we may see as a blatant disregard for the safety of his own child. What is actually going on here? Should social services be called in? Hey, someone call 9-1-1!

While I do not know for sure how Abraham got to this point of absolute surrender to the will of God, I do know that Abraham had questions and times of doubting. What is it about waiting on a promise that leads to doubting? Here are but two of those times:

In the first example, after a period of waiting, we come to Abraham asking God an important question. "But Abram said, 'Sovereign LORD, how can I know that I will gain possession of it'" (Gen. 15:8). Then, in the second example, as we come to Genesis 16, we see Abram, the father of faith, trying to rush God's plan. God has promised to Abram land and a family, and so far, Abram has received neither. So in Genesis 16:1, Abram tries to provide a family for himself rather than trust and wait on God. "Now Sarai, Abram's wife, had borne him no children. But she had an Egyptian slave named Hagar" (Gen. 16:1).

We all set benchmarks, goals, and standards we'd like to meet (Abraham's faith) but realize that, just like a new runner cannot immediately sign up to run a marathon or a start-up business cannot immediately benchmark the annual sales of a mega corporation, we must not get discouraged when we struggle with surrender. The Lord knows our heart. Through our struggles and challenges, we learn and grow, and it's also how our faith is built. Even Abraham had to build his faith muscles.

> The angel of the LORD called to Abraham from heaven a second time and said, "I swear by myself, declares the LORD, that because you have done this and have not withheld your son, your only son, I will surely bless you and make your descendants as numerous as the stars in the sky and as the sand on the seashore. Your descendants will take possession of the cities of their enemies, and through your offspring all nations on earth will be blessed, because you have obeyed me" (Gen. 22:15–18).

Obedience brings blessing. When we are obedient to what God asks us to do, we will be blessed. The above scripture tells the story of how Abraham was blessed from his obedience to lay down Isaac, his only son. For example, when I was asked to leave my career that I loved, the Lord actually gave me the opportunity to lead in a different way, and now to write a book. Guess what? I have always dreamed of writing a book.

In the story of Abraham, he had to come to the place where he willingly gave back to God what was always God's in the first place. After I read this scripture, I began to wonder if I could lay down my children as Abraham had done so willingly. Have you ever thought about that? Isn't it our job to watch over our own children? God said no. He is the only one who can protect and be with your child all the time. You cannot. Release and let God have them. So you see, God is sovereign over everything dear to us.

What am I referring to when I say "white flag"? I am talking about a white flag by what it is known for, surrender. What is God asking you to surrender to Him so you can have victory? I am referring to anything in your life that God is asking you to put down. This includes any idol in your life, that is, anything you have made more important than God. An idol is anything you would have a difficult time letting go of if you had to, or it is something to which you tend to spend a significant amount of time with. It is something you hold tightly to in your heart.

When we think of idols, we think of something we bow down and worship, right? But that is not the case. Most of our idols are perfectly good things. That thing I was holding on to so tightly wasn't anything bad, evil, or wrong. It was something good that had become too important to me. For me, it was my career. How many of you know that God owns everything? For me, this has been such a process. Because it seemed, as soon as I surrendered my idol, I picked it right back up. The Lord asked me to surrender my idol to Him because He said I was holding on too tight to it.

I knew then exactly what the Lord meant. The words were true, and they cut deep. And at the time, I went before the Lord and waved my white flag. But guess what? I stood up, threw the white flag in the trash, and settled in for more achievement and accolades from the business world. While a career was not a bad thing, for me, I had been asked to lead another line of work, and I was having difficulty letting go of my career.

Surrender is a sacrifice. This means it will cost us something. When we are asked to lay down certain things, it is not going to be easy. Surrender admits, "I really have no control. God has all the control, and He is sovereign in all things." Surrender also means we give up the role of playing God in our lives. God is the ruler and master of the universe. And guess what? He is the ruler of your life and everything associated with that. When you get to this point, you get it.

The same can be true of times of crises in our lives. This is when we feel the most out of control, right? I have learned that, once we admit we are weak and surrender it to Him, His grace, and His power to do, it shows up. Wow! His strength is made perfect in my weakness. When we finally surrender and wave our white flags, His power shows up, and we have victory.

"But he said to me, 'My grace is sufficient for you, for my power is made perfect in weakness.' Therefore I will boast all the more gladly about my weaknesses, so that Christ's power may rest on me" (2 Cor. 12:9). During these times, we need to surrender all details to God.

The still, small voice of God and His promises can encourage our step of faith. Once Abraham made the choice to obey and to sacrifice Isaac, God had already made a promise to Him that, through Isaac, He would bless the nations. Abraham knew this, and he also knew the character of God. God is powerful, and He could bring back Isaac from the dead if needed.

Therefore, when God asks us to step out in faith and surrender our Isaac, we work from what we know about the character of God and the promises He has made to us. "God is not human, that he should lie, not a human being, that he should change his mind. Does he speak and then not act? Does he promise and not fulfill" (Num. 23:19). God began showing me, by believing and having faith, He can do the impossible in my situation without doubting releasing power. I challenge you to do the same in your situation, to proclaim that nothing is impossible with God.

During the Exodus, when the Israelites were running from Pharoah and his men, when they got to the Red Sea and seemed to be trapped, they began complaining. "Moses answered the people, 'Do not be afraid. Stand firm and you will see the deliverance the LORD will bring you today. The Egyptians you see today you will never see again. The LORD will fight for you; you need only to be still'" (Ex. 14:13–14).

God often uses times of impossible situations to reveal His glory. "With man this is impossible, but with God all things are possible" (Matt. 19:26). Moses told the Israelites to camp at the Red Sea. Hey, wait a minute. If the Egyptians come, there is no escape. But remember, God will do the impossible and part the Red Sea. But they had to have faith. Moses had to have faith to do this, expecting that God would show up.

How many of you are being asked to camp on the shore for your deliverance? This is in comparison to you being asked to wave your white flag and let God fight your battle. This is your moment of faith. But you have to surrender and let go so God can do his work. "Be still, and know that I am God; I will be exalted among the nations, I will be exalted in the earth" (Ps. 46:10).

Just as we study history to learn from our mistakes and to make positive changes, my prayer is that we can learn something from Abraham's experience. Do you realize that, when we hold tightly, God has a way of showing us we need to let go. This can come in the package of a burden. We were never meant to carry burdens. I have learned that, when we find ourselves in the spin cycle of control, manipulation, and seeking to change things or people, we have made something or someone an idol in our life. And pretty soon, this idol is looking like a burden. Why? We are not God. We play God to our own idols because this is our thing—our career, our work, our car, and our relationship. I tell you this because I have lived this. I carried a burden that almost destroyed me at one time. Will you surrender your burden today? Will you surrender all areas of your life to the lordship of Christ today and receive the victory that He has waiting for you on the shore of your life?

Why is this one little word, surrender, so difficult? We all have dreams, hopes, and plans for ourselves. God may be asking you to surrender to His will and not your own. This is when the rubber hits the road. This is when you must surrender. I believe this is why God tells us to "Humble yourselves, therefore, under God's mighty hand, that he may lift you up in due time. Cast all your anxiety on him because he cares for you. Be alert and of sober mind. Your enemy the devil prowls around like a roaring lion looking for someone to devour" (1 Pet. 5:6–8).

We win when

- we bring the things that we are holding onto tightly and release them to the Lord
- we confess we have been playing the role of God in our own lives by putting on the hats of judge, protector, ruler, controller, problem solver, king, and queen, and
- we surrender all in our lives.

We get the victory. When we confess before the Lord that we have played judge of another by holding onto bitterness and as we release the hurts that others have done to us, I truly believe this is when we find peace. Perfect love casts out fear. Love can heal you. My prayer is you will surrender all that is keeping you from victory.

For Abraham, I can only imagine that there must have been times of smaller faith-building tests before this huge test. So be encouraged if God is asking you to surrender and you are having a hard time doing it. I and all of us struggle because we are all human. My dear friend, I struggle as I write these words. Sometimes, as I had to do, we must ask God to help us. Be encouraged. Strong faith is not built overnight, and neither is surrender. Both are a process.

I have come to realize that, as long as we are looking at the world through our flesh, we will have difficulty surrendering what the Lord is asking us to surrender. I believe that surrender is a choice that we must make. Abraham had a choice that day with Isaac, and He decided to surrender His Isaac. And from that choice, generations are blessed today through the blessing promised Abraham.

However, Abraham had to do something first. He had to be obedient to what God asked him to do, no matter how difficult that was for him. What blessing are you missing by holding onto your Isaac? "Humble yourselves before the Lord, and he will lift you up" (James 4:10).

Because of Jesus's work on the cross, the promises of Isaiah 61 are a personal promise. Claim them as yours! In this same scripture passage, God also promises "a day of vengeance," which is when God will administer justice and avenge us for all of the wrongs done to us forever. Oh, happy day, huh?

In a chapter filled with letting things go, I will also include a section on forgiveness, a crucial part of surrender. In addition, forgiveness is a mandatory part of our journey to new life. We do not have to hold others accountable because God promises to avenge those of His own who are harmed.

> The Spirit of the Sovereign LORD is on me, because the LORD has anointed me to proclaim good news to the poor. He has sent me to bind up the brokenhearted, to proclaim freedom for the captives and release from darkness for the prisoners, to proclaim the year of the LORD's favor and the day of vengeance of our God, to comfort all who mourn, and provide for those who grieve in Zion—to bestow on them a crown of beauty instead of ashes, the oil of joy instead of mourning, and a garment of praise instead of a spirit of despair. They will be called oaks of righteousness, a planting of the LORD for the display of his splendor" (Isa. 61:1–3).

This past weekend, my family baked chocolate muffins. They were light, fluffy, and delicious. But you know the last time we baked some brownies, they turned out dry with no flavor. Why? We had left out an important ingredient, the eggs. New life can become difficult (hard) without blossoms (no beauty) if forgiveness is missing. Forgiveness is like the missing ingredient in the journey. It is essential to new life.

In my moments of healing, I had to forgive others. When I had not released the hurt and pain and forgiven my dad, my life was still impacted from this hurt that had happened many years ago. You see, forgiveness is a vital part of this journey. If we do not heal our past wounds including forgiveness, then when future wounds happen, we just have this new trauma on top of the past trauma. This realization was also a part of my journey.

I love the analogy of a rose or flower, which is new life or new beginnings. You must forgive in order to let go of the past and to progress in your journey to new life. I believe that forgiveness is not just an option on the journey to new life. It is mandatory. Without forgiving the other for the harm caused to you, you are making a decision to carry this person with you each step of your journey. When you do this, your journey is a perpetual struggle. "Bear with each other and forgive one another if any of you has a grievance against someone. Forgive as the Lord forgave you" (Col. 3:13).

When another person hurts you, it can leave you in shock or anger with defense mechanisms ready to build tall walls of self-protection. You might even dream of revenge. These are all normal feelings, and it is okay to feel this way. However, God commands us to forgive. I believe that, when you choose not to forgive, the person who is harmed is you.

One way I describe this is continuing to take steps in the journey, but your steps are heavy. Our world as we knew it seems altered in some way. Of course, this is as unique as each individual situation. But one word is resonating, forgiveness. How do you start? Why would you want to? Forgiveness is a choice, not a feeling. I am not an expert on forgiveness; however, I know how vital this step is in your journey.

I also believe that forgiveness can be a process and will happen at different times, as unique in its timing as each individual. While the ideal time to forgive is immediately, depending on the nature of the offense and how deep the wound is, it can take time. That's okay. Furthermore, things can be compounded when we decide not to forgive. For one, we can find ourselves operating in fear. Oftentimes when we find ourselves afraid of what that another person might do to us, it is because we are holding onto unforgiveness. When we forgive, a myriad of negative emotions and energy leave us, and we feel peace.

For the sake of illustration, I will share a hypothetical example of forgiveness. Let's say you purchase a home in a neighborhood where you have a huge yard. You have always dreamed of having your own yard and a beautiful porch where you can enjoy both privacy and peace. One afternoon, your neighbor begins tossing his leaves into your yard. In addition, he begins long hours of building what looks like deck furniture because he runs a power sander that is extremely loud. It seems this neighbor starts up just when you are sitting on your lovely porch to enjoy a peaceful dinner. You decide to ask this neighbor to not toss his leaves into your yard. You begin to speak behind this person's back and your temper flares more and more every time the power sander starts. Your suburban dreams of peace and tranquility soon turn into a nightmare.

One evening, this neighbor completely humiliates and embarrasses you in front of your other neighbors. This neighbor lies about you and says you are an unfriendly neighbor and that you like to cause trouble for them. You are stunned at how this person turned on you and without reason. The neighbor personally insults your character and shares something extremely confidential about you. You walk away humiliated and stunned for twenty-four hours as you cannot wrap your mind around what just happened.

You have a million things going through your mind at this point. You agree that ultimately, you live a life of quiet desperation hoping somehow this person might relocate. You are a person who cares deeply about how other people see you. This has the ability to ruin your reputation, and you have all sorts of fear that this person will destroy your character so others won't respect you as you feel you are entitled. This person seems to be extremely popular with lots of social gatherings out on the back deck. The people invited appear to be your neighbors. Can you see how fear is entering into this scenario?

You feel angry and humiliated. Although you know you have done nothing wrong, you are in shock. So you have the following things going on here:

- You have fear of this person because he has the potential to ruin your reputation.
- You have anger at this person, so you begin to say mean things about him and to judge him and his motives. This only makes you feel worse.
- You have hurt as your feelings are hurt.

You can't sleep because you are in shock and processing it all. Remember, this is a person you believe has a lot of power. This situation has gotten out of hand and it is now in the hands of the other neighbors who you just imagine are plotting your ruin. So now is the time to make a choice:

- **Choice 1:** You will never speak to that person again and want nothing to do with him. He is very bad. You continue to fear that he will ruin your reputation and your need for peace and tranquility. This will move you into bitterness and resentment.
- **Choice 2:** You will take the entire matter to the Lord.

In this case, you choose to take the matter to the Lord and ask Him what to do. So you asked the Lord. First, He leads you to do something nice for this person. So you decided to consider what that might be and to act on it. Second, you took a walk, and as you trod along, you acknowledged and shared with Jesus the hurt and anger you felt at this person. You asked the Lord to heal this hurt. You also acknowledged your fear of what this person might do to ruin you.

So at this point, you have surrendered the hurt, acknowledged the pain, and allowed Jesus to heal it. In addition, you have stepped out and done something kind for this person. (There's a caveat with this. Ask the Lord if this is something He wants you to do. Sometimes this might not be the right thing to do.) And you have confessed your sin of anger toward this person and asked God to forgive you.

So finally you choose to forgive the person, and you have surrendered the person to God. You left this person in God's hands to avenge. So if God needs to avenge you, God will do it. This may or may not lead to reconciliation.

The point of all of this is that forgiveness is a must in order for us to move on in our lives. When we do not forgive, we say that person owes us something. And guess what? We are the ones who get hurt and bogged down with the burden. When we do not forgive, we take that person with us everywhere. It is like saying, "Hey, you! Jump on my back, and I will carry you with me wherever I go." Think about it. In addition, when we don't forgive, roots of bitterness grow, leading to all sorts of other issues and further sin. So it is best to forgive quickly.

The result in this scenario might be that your fear of this neighbor will be gone. That you will no longer find yourself talking about them and all of the things you imagine they are doing to irritate you. You might even enjoy that porch for once. You rest in knowing that God is sovereign and no one can destroy His plans. Also, in this case, there could have been reconciliation of the relationship. However, even without that (and in some cases that won't happen), you can, on your end, work these steps and receive peace. Are you ready to wave your white flag?

In my own personal journey, I was able to forgive and move on from a long-term rift in a relationship. I have learned that, when I forgive the person who hurt me and I release him or her to God, then I recognize that God has sovereignty over all matters. When I had unconfessed sin in my heart, I found myself afraid of the person. I would go out of my way to avoid that person at all costs. I also was afraid of what that person was saying about me behind my back. It was so freeing after I forgave because those fear feelings went away. In my case, I was actually able to take a gift to that other person. "There is no fear in love. But perfect love drives out fear, because fear has to do with punishment. The one who fears is not made perfect in love" (1 John 4:18).

Have you heard this before, "Perfect love casts out fear"? Well, this is exactly what happens. The fear of that person and what he or she might do goes away. We then rest in the sovereignty of God. God is bigger than any person or thing, and He is the ultimate authority. People may choose to do or say mean things. We must surrender this to the Lord. From this, you no longer fear that other person. This fear is replaced with faith that God has this situation.

Surrendering/Letting Go Is Always the Key to Victory

I pray that you will release and surrender your hurt, your loss, and your pain to God so the healing power of Jesus can touch those broken places. I pray the Lord has been revealing some situations and/or some people that need surrendering. God is sovereign and controls all things. When we surrender to Him, we can rest in knowing that His perfect purpose will prevail. As we release, there is victory. Are you ready to surrender and give it to God? If so, you will find joy and peace in the surrender.

And so I ask you today: will you surrender and wave your white flag? Will you release any burden you have been carrying? Will you allow God to be God even if it means you have to let go of your dream? Will you surrender your "even ifs"? Will you remove the boulder on your back and accept that God has this? Can we do this together? As we say, "Father, your will and not my own."

Remember that surrendering is a process. When I finally waved my white flag, a blessing was released in the spirit. I will never forget the day. I share this with you because, as we wave our white flags in surrender, God's blessings are released. Something was released in the spiritual realm that day. Just like Abraham's obedience and laying down his Isaac, God released the blessing to Abraham that extends down to every person who receives Jesus as Lord and Savior. Now that is what I call ultimate victory!

CHAPTER 10

Joy of the Redeemed

Ralph Waldo Emerson once said, "All I have seen teaches me to trust the Creator for all I have not seen."

For this last message, I am going to do something a little different. I am going to reverse the sequence of events. In the movies, this is called reverse chronology.

It was a beautiful day on the beach of Isle of Palms, South Carolina. On this particular day, I was on a mission. I had made a decision that I needed to take a walk on the beach and release some pain to the Lord. I chose that day to share with the Lord the pain and the suffering I had experienced on this journey. It was my day to ask Jesus to heal any traces of unhealed hurt.

As I shared my wounds with Jesus and allowed His light to touch those broken places, the Lord very unexpectedly began to reveal His great love for me. It was almost as if the Lord were giving me meaningful gifts and surprises along the shore. Before I knew it, I was smiling and feeling very lighthearted. It seemed as if I didn't have a care in the world as I found one surprise of blessing after another. My first surprise was a perfect sand dollar. This was a real treasure to me because I have never found one before. Then I found a shell shaped like a butterfly with a broken wing. I released all of the pain that day, and I found such excitement and joy walking in the water. I felt the love of a God who shared with me that He had been in all of the pain and He was using it for good. It was part of the big picture that we often cannot see. He allowed me to feel His love for me and His genuine concern about what I had suffered. I knew He was a faithful, loving God, despite the painful experiences. And suffering is part of His eternal plan.

How can I express the feeling of joy unspeakable that I felt at that moment when I realized that I was on the mind of the God of the universe and He had been with me in every single detail and each single moment of my pain? I really feel that the Lord allowed me to know this so I can tell you that He is with you as well. God is with you every single detail of your journey, no matter what you have experienced. That was a day I will always treasure and one of which I will never forget.

The joy I felt on that day was something I have never before experienced in my life. For you see, I had been working on this particular message for a couple years because I could not find the joy. But somehow that day, I knew that this experience, the joy, was the joy of the redeemed. God shared His redeeming plan for all of the hurt and suffering I had experienced. What a beautiful gift I received that day. I had been searching for the joy all of these years, and in these messages, however, the joy eluded me. I could not find it anywhere. I could never understand how there could be joy in suffering. You see, I had been looking for it in my circumstances. I found the joy that day, as if it were beautiful sparkles of glitter falling upon me on the sand.

> "Comfort, comfort my people," says your God. "Speak tenderly to Jerusalem, and proclaim to her that her hard service has been completed, that her sin has been paid for, that she has received from the LORD's hand double for all her sins. A voice of one calling: 'In the wilderness prepare the way for the LORD; make straight in the desert a highway for our God. Every valley shall be raised up, every mountain and hill made low; the rough ground shall become level, the rugged places a plain. And the glory of the LORD will be revealed, and all people will see it together. For the mouth of the LORD has spoken'" (Isa. 40:1–5).

Have you ever had one of those mornings when the day just hits you as soon as you put your feet on the floor? Well, recently I had one such morning. Upon handling the matter at hand, I returned to have my quiet devotion time. As I opened my Bible for my morning devotion, along with my much needed first cup of coffee, I turned direct to the following scripture:

> Awake, awake, Zion, clothe yourself with strength! Put
> on your garments of splendor, Jerusalem, the holy city.
> The uncircumcised and defiled will not enter you again.
> Shake off your dust; rise up, sit enthroned, Jerusalem.
> Free yourself from the chains on your neck, Daughter
> Zion, now a captive (Isa. 52:1–2).

I want you to know that this is just one example of how the Lord has worked as He gave me these messages. "Awake, awake." I woke up this morning as if someone had awakened me. As with every moment of our lives, it was a precise time. And so you see, there is a precise time when all of our chains will fall away, and we too will be free. "I sought the LORD, and he answered me; he delivered me from all my fears" (Ps. 34:4).

This journey would be missing something if I did not include two words, deliverance and salvation. God has a day of deliverance for you and me in each trial that we encounter. And though we may have to wait for it, God is with us each and every step of our journey. He is right there, giving us grace, strength, rest, hope, comfort, and, yes, restoration. He provides all of this so we can put one foot out in front of the other and walk our journey. And, yes, like me this morning, sometimes we have to just keep moving, even without our coffee.

You see, deliverance and salvation have a time-stamp on them. It is a date with a time. Ultimately, when Jesus returns, He will make all wrongs right. But for now, He is right here with you, providing you comfort, strength, hope, and grace. Jesus loves you, and it is my prayer that this book will show you the power of Jesus crucified as well as the day of deliverance that awaits you in your current circumstance, whatever that might be. God promises to exchange your ashes for beauty, your spirit of heaviness with the oil of joy, your mourning with comfort, your broken heart with healing, and your captivity with freedom. And your spirit of despair will become a garment of praise. You see, this is how much God loves you. "For God so loved the world that he gave his one and only Son, that whoever believes in him shall not perish but have eternal life" (John 3:16).

"The thief comes only to steal and kill and destroy; I have come that they may have life, and have it to the full" (John 10:10). God does that with our lives. He gives us a second chance. He always redeems the brokenness.

> How beautiful on the mountains are the feet of those who bring good news, who proclaim peace, who bring good tidings, who proclaim salvation, who say to Zion, "Your God reigns!" Listen! Your watchmen lift up their voices; together they shout for joy. When the LORD returns to Zion, they will see it with their own eyes. Burst into songs of joy together, you ruins of Jerusalem, for the LORD has comforted his people, he has redeemed Jerusalem (Isa. 52:7–9).

What does joy mean? Webster's Dictionary 1913 defines joy as "to rejoice; to be glad; to delight; to exult. The passion or emotion excited by the acquisition or expectation of good; pleasurable feelings or emotions caused by success, good fortune, and the like, or by a rational prospect of possessing what we love or desire; gladness; exhilaration of spirits; delight."

What does redeem mean? Webster's Dictionary 1913 defines redeem as "to ransom, liberate, or rescue from captivity or bondage, or from any obligation or liability to suffer or to be forfeited, by paying a price or ransom; to ransom; to rescue; to recover; as, to redeem a captive, a pledge, and the like."

God has a day of deliverance and salvation. What promises has God made to you about your situation? Hold onto these promises. What can we learn in times of waiting?

The desert and the parched land will be glad; the wilderness will rejoice and blossom. Like the crocus, it will burst into bloom; it will rejoice greatly and shout for joy. The glory of Lebanon will be given to it, the splendor of Carmel and Sharon; they will see the glory of the LORD, the splendor of our God. Strengthen the feeble hands, steady the knees that give way; say to those with fearful hearts, "Be strong, do not fear; your God will come, he will come with vengeance; with divine retribution he will come to save you" (Isa. 35:14).

When bad news, trauma, or crises hit us, like a train rolling through our lives, we stare at and look around, and everything seems destroyed—our dreams, our plans, and our hopes. We wonder how life can ever continue. How can we go on? Everything seems completely destroyed like a hopeless desert, void of any life. As we sit in the shock and the ashes, Jesus weeps with us. Because of Jesus and the power of the cross, we have hope as He holds out His hand to pick us up and carry us. Out of the ashes and the dry desert, we take one step at a time, not because we want to, but because we have to. We begin this journey to new life. Prophetically, full restoration will happen one day, and the entire desert will become like Eden, as Isaiah 35:12 promises. But today, because of the power of the cross, new life does blossom.

I have received reminders of the prophetic promises of Isaiah 35. One day as I was reading a commentary on this scripture, suddenly the wind blew a flowerpot of roses over on the porch. Several rosebuds were tossed upon the floor. On another occasion, the plants at my home died during a hot and dry season. Amazingly, one morning I awoke to find some of them blooming. I am reminded that God takes the dry desert of our lives and redeems, restoring it. I love the analogy of a rose or flower that is new life, new beginnings. God redeemed me from my bad choices and sin and gave me a second chance. He will do the same for you. God always redeems you no matter what you've done or the mistakes you've made. You literally get to start fresh.

How many of you know that there is a day of salvation, of

deliverance? But what gets us is when time goes by and nothing seems to change. During these times, hold onto the promise that God made you. You know when God has promised you something. One thing I know is that all of the darkness, brokenness, and suffering will end one day. The desert will be transformed into new life. Does this make the journey easy? No. Is the journey painful? Yes. Is it excruciating? Yes. But I am here to testify that even what we are going through now will all be turned around. And look! Who is it that I see on the horizon?

"Who is this coming from Edom, from Bozrah, with his garments stained crimson? Who is this, robed in splendor, striding forward in the greatness of his strength? 'It is I, proclaiming victory, mighty to save'" (Isa. 63:1).

"Oh Lord, you took up my case. You redeemed my life. You have seen, oh Lord, the wrong done to me. Uphold my cause" (Lam. 3:58–59). When someone hurts or causes harm to you, God promises to fight this battle for you and to avenge you. God fights the battle, and He is stronger than anything that another person did to you. Sometimes another person's sin can cause you to suffer. This is not your fault. You are innocent, and God promises to avenge and to deliver you. "The LORD is close to the brokenhearted and saves those who are crushed in spirit" (Psalm 34:18). You are God's beloved child, and He will avenge you for anyone who hurts you. You are only asked to surrender this hurt to the Lord and to forgive the one who hurt you. God will do the rest.

In suffering, there can be treasure. It can build your faith and bring you closer to others. It can lead to the healing of present and past wounds. It can allow you to see God's grace and His power of deliverance and salvation, comfort, restoration, healing, and peace so this might be shared with others. God is sovereign, all-powerful, omnipotent, and omniscient. He is ruler and master of the entire universe. He is a loving God, but He is also holy and loves us too much to allow us to continue in our sin.

Let's recount some scriptures from our journey.

"The Spirit of the Sovereign LORD is on me, because the LORD has anointed me to proclaim good news to the poor. He has sent me to bind up the brokenhearted, to proclaim freedom for the captives and release from darkness for the prisoners, to proclaim the year of the LORD's favor" (Isa. 61:1).

As you recall, Jesus stopped here in the temple when He read the scroll before beginning His ministry on earth. However, the scripture continues as follows,

> And the day of vengeance of our God, to comfort all who mourn, and provide for those who grieve in Zion— to bestow on them a crown of beauty instead of ashes, the oil of joy instead of mourning, and a garment of praise instead of a spirit of despair. They will be called oaks of righteousness, a planting of the LORD for the display of his splendor (Isa. 61:2–3).

Remember, God promises to avenge those who are harmed. "I delight greatly in the LORD; my soul rejoices in my God. For he has clothed me with garments of salvation and arrayed me in a robe of his righteousness, as a bridegroom adorns his head like a priest, and as a bride adorns herself with her jewels" (Isa. 61:10).

We are robed in a robe of righteousness. Because of Jesus's death for our sins on the cross, when God looks at us, He sees Jesus. We are the righteousness of Christ Jesus. No matter what is done to us or what we do, nothing changes this robe of righteousness.

Let's reflect on joy for a moment. The Bible speaks of joy in a few ways. First of all, joy is one of the fruits of the Spirit, which we receive as followers of the Lord Jesus. "But the fruit of the Spirit is love, joy, peace, forbearance, kindness, goodness, faithfulness, gentleness and self-control. Against such things there is no law" (Gal. 5:22–23).

Second, remember the joy we feel when we realize who we are in Christ. Therefore, joy is also what we experience when we realize who we are in Christ, the robe of righteousness. Do you think we can experience joy when we realize that Jesus is with us in our pain?

The foundational scripture for this book has been Isaiah 61. God promises an exchange. When we give him our ashes, for example, our burdens, our suffering, our loss, and our pain—and the list goes on and on and is as specific as each specific individual—He promises to give us something better. For the purposes of this message, we are using the example of joy. You ask how we can possibly have joy in the midst of destruction, suffering, and heartache.

All we have to do is look at the news reports all around us. What about the stories of the people who have lost everything and yet have joy? As I read about the stories of the people who have lost everything, I wonder how there can possibly be joy. They have literally lost everything. However, there was joy in the midst.

How about Paul and Silas in the Bible? They were in jail, and they were singing songs. In the midst of their great crisis, they were singing songs of joy. They had more joy than many people who have everything, who have so much, and yet there is grumbling and complaining. I am speaking to myself now. How is this possible? We have everything, and yet we are frustrated at best. I have heard stories of people who were going through the unimaginable and yet they were singing songs of joy.

One morning, I awoke from a very vivid dream, one that has stuck with me. I don't have dreams like this often so I decided to write it down. In the dream, I was sitting on a hill.

As I looked around, I said, "The destruction is so great."

At what seemed to be the end of the dream, the clouds started shifting and moving around very quickly. For some reason, it seemed like it was on a stage. When the clouds subsided, I saw several dancers, dancing in unison. From this dream, I felt that this reflected how God promises to turn our mourning into dancing. It was about redemption.

What about the dream I had? I saw great destruction, and I said, "The destruction is so great." Then the stage opened up, and people were dancing around on the stage. I believe the people in the stories I have read of this great joy in horrible circumstances, as well as this dream, had experienced something greater than them or their circumstance. They had experienced and met Jesus. When we encounter Jesus, we are never the same. His encounter does not change what happened to us, but He exchanges our ashes for beauty. We can have joy in the midst of extreme suffering.

Are not these stories that we read of those experiencing a crisis that would leave the very strongest worn, afraid, and hopeless? But listen to me, my friend, the God of hope came. The God of redemption laid His hand on them, and we see the joy of the redeemed. And so I ask you: where is your hope? Our only hope comes from the Lord.

What is restoration? Webster's Dictionary 1913 defines restoration as "the act of restoring or bringing back to a former place, station, or condition; the fact of being restored; renewal; reestablishment; as, the restoration of friendship between enemies; the restoration of peace after war. The state of being restored; recovery of health, strength, etc.; as, restoration from sickness."

I have learned that restoration is a process. The inner healings we experience are as real as the power of the blood of the cross that made them possible. Yes, absolutely, we are being restored. The Lord restores His servants, but it has to be done in His way and His time. In addition, full restoration for all matters of all people through the ages that have been taken will not fully be restored until the day of vengeance when Jesus Christ returns as the Lion of Judah and makes all things new. As humans, we live in a time-centered world. God does not. Prophetically God is revealing the restoration to us. He is drawing us to Him and telling what He is doing on the earth. Prophetic words are often future-oriented, so you see it can be easy to get wrapped up in the time factor of our human nature and become frustrated.

God says, "See, I am doing a new thing! Now it springs up; do you not perceive it? I am making a way in the wilderness and streams in the wasteland" (Isa. 43:19). As we perceive, we must recognize what is now prior to Christ's return and what is later upon His return. God is announcing His plans of restoration of all, and we are seeing degrees of it on the earth. Praise God. But ultimately, the final and complete restoration of all things will occur when Jesus Christ returns. The world will be a very dark place when Jesus returns.

And remember that God is still good even if the restoration doesn't arrive on our time table or look like we imagined it to look. God will have mercy on who He has mercy. We must be willing to humble ourselves and realize that His ways are not our own. Again, God always restores His servants, but it has to be done in His way and His timing.

God has promised, "Never will I leave you; never will I forsake you" (Heb. 13:5).

These promises do not mean that bad things won't happen to us. They mean that we can count on God's presence as we face all things that life brings our way. Even in the midst of terrible circumstances, God is with us, saving us in ways we may not even be able to comprehend at the time. I searched so intensely for joy during my journey, but it always eluded me. I couldn't find it because I failed to realize that God was with me every single step of the way and He was redeeming things in ways in which I had no comprehension. I was looking for the joy in what I could see. I couldn't find the purpose in my pain.

Jesus said, "I have told you these things, so that in me you may have peace. In this world you will have trouble. But take heart! I have overcome the world" (John 16:33).

Redemption may be future-oriented. It is about God taking your pain and turning it into something good and you getting to see that. For example, my spirit is redeemed, and I have a home in heaven. Let's use the example of your mortgage loan. Let's say you receive a copy of your deed in the mail one day and it is marked "paid in full." Would you be overcome with elation that someone paid off your mortgage for you and you now own the house? Would you be overcome with delight that you no longer have this debt and can now use that money to have more expendable income? That is what Jesus did for us on the cross. He paid a debt that we could never pay. Your debt is paid in full! In addition, God promises, "And we know that in all things God works for the good of those who love him, who have been called according to his purpose" (Rom. 8:28).

Restoration is about the renewal and the recovery. God restores and heals our wounds. He heals relationships, broken hearts, and shame. He teaches us that we are dressed in that beautiful dress or garment. We are able to move on, having grown stronger in the process. God is our strength, and He wants to restore all that the enemy has taken from you. God promises to turn it all around, the years that the locust took and were lost. But this is a process. And there are many examples of losses that we have experienced in this life, such as the loss of loved ones that we will not see in this life. The one thing, however, that can never be taken from us is hope.

> Why do you complain, Jacob? Why do you say, Israel, "My way is hidden from the LORD; my cause is disregarded by my God"? Do you not know? Have you not heard? The LORD is the everlasting God, the Creator of the ends of the earth. He will not grow tired or weary, and his understanding no one can fathom. He gives strength to the weary and increases the power of the weak. Even youths grow tired and weary, and young men stumble and fall; but those who hope in the LORD will renew their strength. They will soar on wings like eagles; they will run and not grow weary, they will walk and not be faint (Isa. 40:27–31).

I'm challenging you today to recognize that the difficult times, the challenging times, and the darkest of times can actually be as shimmers of joy in the darkness, as hope arises and the joy of the redeemed shines bright. "The LORD is my strength and my shield; my heart trusts in him, and he helps me. My heart leaps for joy, and with my song I praise him" (Ps. 28:7).

God is about to do something miraculous. He is about to lift you out of the ashes and watch you jump for joy! When He does, you will know it was Him. There is a positive correlation between the level of joy we experience and the amount of time we spend in relationship with the Lord. God can take the brokenness, the pain, and the sorrow and use it to redeem, restore, and heal you. And He can use it to do the same to those who are watching from the sidelines.

We are all longing for home. This earth is not our home. Have you ever met a person who was full of joy, yet he or she had struggles and life wasn't perfect? He or she gets it! Joy is not based on circumstances. I believe that these people know in their hearts that full restoration is coming. And they expect it. We can be assured of this one thing. On this earth, we will have trouble. Jesus said, "I have told you these things, so that in me you may have peace. In this world you will have trouble. But take heart! I have overcome the world" (John 16:33). Because of Jesus, we too are overcomers.

The Lord gave me a gift that day as I walked on the beach as He revealed to me a deeper level of the meaning of the joy of the redeemed. This gift is one that He wants me to share. You see, this gift was not for me alone. It was for anyone reading these words. I want to share this gift with you. God wants you to know that He is with you in every single detail of your heartache. He will redeem your pain and your heartache as well. But He wants you to share with Him all of it, every detail of it, so the light of Jesus can shine on the broken places of your heart with His healing presence. I pray that you too will experience this joy, which is not defined by your circumstance.

Also our joy is not because our situations change, though they may. It is something much deeper. We can pull that joy out of a place in us. The joy of the Lord, the joy of the redeemed, is a part of us. My prayer is for you to experience this deeper level of joy.

And so, when I was walking on the beach that day, the Lord said he was redeeming the pain because it was going to help other people. He was with me each and every step of the way. I felt the joy, as I knew He had been there the entire time. And He allowed me to feel that He had been with me the entire time. It was as if I were given a gift of returning to a moment of time to once again experience my deep anguish, but this time I was seeing the Lord right there in that particular moment. This brought me great joy. That was the day the Lord allowed me to finally find the joy I had been searching for years to find. You see, I could not find the joy because my focus was on me and not the bigger picture. It was the joy of what God would bring from the brokenness. It doesn't mean that there wasn't pain or that I wasn't hurt.

And so you see, I learned a valuable lesson about joy. I realized that the joy of the redeemed is not a feeling based on circumstances. Thank you, Jesus, for the journey, for showing me that you have carried me every step of the way, and that you always redeem what the enemy meant for evil. And you will use it to help others. Thank you for the joy of a redeemed life.

There is beauty from ashes. There is praise for a spirit of despair. There is joy for mourning.

Today, as I stand and view the place I have grown to love, I take my first step onto a path I've walked hundreds of times, but this time I sense this route is leading elsewhere. Does this mean I will forget about this part of my journey? No, never. I will never forget this portion. I will never forget the joy I experienced that day on the beach. I will never forget because Jesus has been walking with me each and every step of my journey. I would not trade my pain if it meant I would lose the joy I experienced on that beach that day.

And as I stand at the end of this particular portion of my journey, I pass this along to you. As you take Jesus's hand, I pray that you will recognize the joy along the way. I may have found it at the end of this particular portion of my journey. So please remember this: each time you receive comfort, strength, rest, restoration, redemption, peace, grace, mercy, love, and joy, release these sequins of hope to someone else.

> He said, "Surely they are my people, children who will be true to me"; and so he became their Savior. In all their distress he too was distressed, and the angel of his presence saved them. In his love and mercy he redeemed them; he lifted them up and carried them all the days of old (Isa. 63:8–9).

CHAPTER 11

Sequins of Hope

This chapter is a treasure chest collection of lessons learned in the journey. While you will have read these throughout the journey, I thought this might be a great way to pull out these sequins of hope as you start your personal journey. This will help you to enjoy this book without having to take notes or get bogged down in the details. My prayer also is that reading the details shared in my personal journey of how God gave hope, healing, and restoration to me will encourage you as you go through your journey to new life. You can use this chapter to read again as you watch the Holy Spirit work in your life.

This also allows more freedom for others who might use this as an additional resource or learning tool. This chapter can also serve as a leader's guide for group study. In addition, because the original messages of hope and restoration are included in the text of this entire book, these Holy Spirit-inspired messages could be shared with others within a ministry group setting. Remember that the healing and restoration process is different for each person. And I must add that each individual's journey will be as unique as each individual.

God taught me so much in my journey. God reminded me that ultimately the Holy Spirit is our counselor. "But the Advocate, the Holy Spirit, whom the Father will send in my name, will teach you all things and will remind you of everything I have said to you" (John 14:26). The Holy Spirit, as my teacher, began to share with me the process of healing my wounds. And through that, I would share with others who are hurting how the Holy Spirit is our helper in the healing process.

Please note that I am not a licensed clinical social worker (LCSW) or a psychologist. I am only a servant of the Lord, sharing what has worked for me. This is not in any manner a suggestion that you should not seek professional-level counseling. I am an advocate for professional counseling and have benefited from it myself. What I share is a journey with the hope that it may help others. The main point is God wants to give you hope and to restore you. He is all about restoration, healing, and redemption. God never leaves us in our brokenness. He is holding out His hand for you. Will you take His hand?

Because of Jesus's work on the cross, the promises of Isaiah 61 are a personal promise. Claim them as yours! God also promises a day of vengeance, which is when God will administer justice and avenge us for all of the wrongs done throughout generations.

> The Spirit of the Sovereign LORD is on me, because the LORD has anointed me to proclaim good news to the poor. He has sent me to bind up the brokenhearted, to proclaim freedom for the captives and release from darkness for the prisoners, to proclaim the year of the LORD's favor and the day of vengeance of our God, to comfort all who mourn, and provide for those who grieve in Zion—to bestow on them a crown of beauty instead of ashes, the oil of joy instead of mourning, and a garment of praise instead of a spirit of despair. They will be called oaks of righteousness, a planting of the LORD for the display of his splendor (Isa. 61:1–3).

Who You Are in Christ

"Therefore, there is now no condemnation for those who are in Christ Jesus" (Rom. 8:1). Romans 8:31–39 says,

What, then, shall we say in response to these things? If God is for us, who can be against us? He who did not spare his own Son, but gave him up for us all—how will he not also, along with him, graciously give us all things? Who will bring any charge against those whom God has chosen? It is God who justifies. Who then is the one who condemns? No one. Christ Jesus who died—more than that, who was raised to life—is at the right hand of God and is also interceding for us. Who shall separate us from the love of Christ? Shall trouble or hardship or persecution or famine or nakedness or danger or sword? As it is written: "For your sake we face death all day long; we are considered as sheep to be slaughtered." No, in all these things we are more than conquerors through him who loved us. For I am convinced that neither death nor life, neither angels nor demons, neither the present nor the future, nor any powers, neither height nor depth, nor anything else in all creation, will be able to separate us from the love of God that is in Christ Jesus our Lord.

An Overview of the Process

"I delight greatly in the LORD; my soul rejoices in my God. For he has clothed me with garments of salvation and arrayed me in a robe of his righteousness, as a bridegroom adorns his head like a priest, and as a bride adorns herself with her jewels" (Isa. 61:10).

This promise is a scripture of hope. It is the first sequin of hope. It is to be used at the beginning. Because of what Jesus did on the cross and His shed blood, when God looks at us, He sees Jesus. He sees us in a beautiful robe of righteousness. Through making this an art project, to imagine what this robe looks like for you personally will help seal this truth for you. God sees us as such. This is the essence of who you are. And so began the process of visualizing and imagining a personal robe of righteousness.

Next, recognize any false beliefs or lies that are contrary to who God says you are, yet another sequin. Please note that at times these lies can come to light by statements made out loud or a thought that simply does not line up in agreement with who God says you are or about the situation. If this happens, ask the Lord for the theory of why you said that statement. He is faithful, and He will share with you. Journaling and sharing in the light of Jesus brings healing. Once the lie is exposed, you take the falsehood and allow the Holy Spirit to share what the thought process is that serves as fuel to the lie. Again, journaling helps. This lie is then replaced with facts that are true, God's truth and what His Word says. Throughout this process, sharing of all of the pain (giving the pain to Jesus), opening up the wounds, and allowing the light of Jesus to enter brings healing to these wounds. Do you notice another sequin here? This lie is replaced with facts that were true, God's truth and what His Word says. Do you notice another sequin here?

Then continue reading these messages (found in the text of this book) of God's truth as a reminder of the fact of being in a robe of righteousness and absolutely nothing changes this fact. The healing comes from the process of realizing who you are in Christ (the dress/garment and nothing that happens to us defines us) + Holy Spirit revealing any lies you may have made when you were hurt + the enemy lies being replaced with the truth (God's truth)

And ultimately sharing all of the pain and opening your wounds to the healing power of the blood of Jesus brings healing to your wounds. Then the dress/garment/visual aid is further solidified for you. You will finally get it and believe it from your heart, not just your head. At this point, I have lost count of the many sequins of hope. As part of this process, the Lord revealed to me the process of healing hurts that are in our hearts, sometimes from decades ago. This journey of hope, healing, and restoration is my gift to you.

And so we begin the process of moving our head knowledge to our hearts so we can believe the truth of who we are in Christ. Christ died and shed His blood to heal, redeem, and restore you.

The Homework Assignment

This week for homework, begin to create a garment of salvation, a robe of righteousness. This will be a visual aid of who you are in Christ. What causes us to not see ourselves this way? Abuse, sin, and things that are done to us create shame, distorting the truth about us. The enemy deceives us into believing lies.

You are robed in a robe of righteousness. Nothing changes this. Things that happen to you do not define you. Nothing changes this robe. You are the righteousness of Christ Jesus. This is the essence of who you are once you accept Jesus's finished work on the cross.

This assignment purpose is to have each person begin to imagine who he or she is and to design a dress, garment, or other visual aid to use as a reminder of who he or she is. It is a tangible project that will be a constant reminder so there is no doubt as the enemy may attempt to make the individual feel this is not true. As with anything, it takes practice and time for this to become solid in your heart and to know beyond a shadow of a doubt that this is true. Over time, this project will be a visual reminder of this truth.

To summarize, this is a process of getting head knowledge to heart knowledge, really getting it. When you get it that who you are in Christ does not change when things are done to you and that these things do not stick to you, there is joy. As you recognize any lies you have been believing, you will begin the process of replacing these falsehoods with truth. As you allow the Jesus to heal the wounds, then the dress/garment is further solidified for you. You will finally get it and believe it from your heart, not just your head.

The Exclamation Point

"But the Advocate, the Holy Spirit, whom the Father will send in my name, will teach you all things and will remind you of everything I have said to you" (John 14:26). "I delight greatly in the LORD; my soul rejoices in my God. For he has clothed me with garments of salvation and arrayed me in a robe of his righteousness, as a bridegroom adorns his head like a priest, and as a bride adorns herself with her jewels" (Isa. 61:10).

This promise is the beginning of healing past wounds. I share this scripture with a message that, because of Jesus's work on the cross, when God looks at you, He sees Jesus. He sees you in a beautiful robe of righteousness. I ask you "What does your dress/garment look like?" This is the essence of who you are. Please accept this and begin the process of seeing yourself in this beautiful dress/garment.

Next, the Holy Spirit may reveal to you something that needs healing. It can come in statements, triggers, what I call "jot down" moments, or however means that the Lord reveals to you personally. This is as unique as each individual. For example, something as innocent as a statement saying "I am a failure" is significant. If a statement is made that is obviously not centered in God's truth, begin asking the Lord what is this about. And the Holy Spirit will lead you to the truth.

The Holy Spirit will begin to reveal to you any lies that you have been believing. Again this information comes from the Holy Spirit. Each person is unique in his or her stories, but my emphasis is on your relationship with Jesus and in sharing your pain and opening your wounds to the healing light of Jesus. Healing is a lifelong journey, and the Lord will reveal wounds that need His healing touch in His timing.

"Shout for joy, you heavens; rejoice, you earth; burst into song, you mountains! For the LORD comforts his people and will have compassion on his afflicted ones" (Isa. 49:13).

Case Study of a Journey

It was a Saturday afternoon, and I began sharing with Mark about a particular afternoon from my childhood. Before I share this story, I want to say that I would not trade my childhood because it made me the person that I am today. The Lord revealed to me that my dad had suffered abuse in his life and through my journey of understanding this, I was able to understand him which brought both forgiveness and healing to me. Anyhow, on with the story. I had just gotten home after school, and I was eating dinner. My dad always picked on me when I got off the bus after school. I remember not wanting to get off the bus in the afternoon. This particular day, I'd had enough. I was sitting and eating my dinner when my dad just kept picking on me. Something came over me, and I threw my food across the room at him. And then before I knew it, we were arguing.

I told him that day, "Do not ever pick on me like this again."

After I said this, I remember feeling very guilty. I recall confessing this sin to the Lord when it happened.

Mark's first words were, "You are still very angry."

I was shocked, but Mark was correct. I had not healed from that day.

Mark said, "That was a defining moment for you. You weren't going to let him do that to you anymore."

It was a defining moment in my life; however, I had what I call a "jot down" moment that day. Upon realizing that I was still angry about that day, I did something different this time. I began to journal what happened that day. I took this before the Lord to ask Him to tell me why I was still so angry about that day. I have learned that, when you have a moment like this, it helps to get your thoughts on paper.

The Lord began to show me that this goes deeper than just writing words on a paper. It was deeper because these feelings would later be shared with Jesus in prayer and these wounds would be opened so His light could heal them. So I began writing every detail.

Once complete, I took the words that I wrote to Jesus and shared my thoughts and feelings, all of it. As I began to share all that I could recall of the painful event, the Holy Spirit revealed the lies, and the truth came during this process. Once the lie is exposed, you take the falsehood and allow the Holy Spirit to share what the thought process was that served as fuel to the lie. Again, journaling helps. This lie is then replaced with facts that are true, God's truth and what His Word says. Ultimately sharing these wounds and all of the pain with Jesus and allowing His light to touch those wounds brings healing.

In the example of the unexpected healing:

- **The thought process that fueled the lie:** I am hurt. I made a promise to myself that no one, including my dad, would ever treat me this way again. So without realizing it at the time, I built a tough wall of self-protection around me.
- **The lie was revealed:** All people are like my dad, so I must protect myself.
- **God's truth:** My dad's behavior was wrong; however, this had to do with his behavior, not me. While the behavior was wrong, this was separate from him as a person. He was created by God and is a loved and valuable human being. All people are not like my dad's behavior. In this process, the exposing to the light of Jesus healed these wounds, and in the process, I forgave my dad.

In addition, as you open up your wounds and share your pain with Jesus, He may take you back in time. For example, the Lord took me back in my memory, and I could literally smell the house I grew up in. And as I cried and felt the pain as if I were still a little girl (as this was the opening of my wounds and exposing them to the light of Jesus), the healing power of Jesus healed my heart. I, in turn, expressed my anger at my dad as if he were in the room. I pretended he was sitting in a chair in my kitchen. I shared everything I was thinking and feeling. I held nothing back. And you know what? This led to my wanting to forgive and hug my dad. I realized that I had formed an opinion of my dad that was not correct. His behavior most likely came from hurt he had experienced in his life that had nothing to do with me. I was healed.

As a result, I became softer toward others in my relationships. Who was present with me that day in my healing of this past wound? Jesus, myself, and my journal. Please note that the Holy Spirit will reveal to you the specifics of your healing so you don't have to strive to figure things out.

So you see, it was a twofold process of healing. First, I had a "jot down" moment. I recognized that I should not be still angry and began to question why I was still fuming after all of these years about that one day. Second, I took it before the Lord (because journaling helps) and asked Him why I was feeling this way. God showed me that I had made a promise that day that "no one would ever treat me that way ever again." In my heart, I categorized anyone who was close to me as being this way, the lie. The falsehood took root when my dad hurt me that day. I began believing the lie that day. I made a promise to myself that no one, including my dad, would ever treat me this way again. I replaced this with the truth. My dad's behavior was wrong; however, this had to do with his behavior, not me. While the behavior was wrong, this was separate from him as a person. He was created by God and is a loved and valuable human being. All people are not like my dad. In this process, the exposing to the light of Jesus healed these wounds, and in the process, I forgave my dad.

In the second example, I was experiencing a trigger, which is when something reminds you of a past event (unhealed) so you overreact when it happens. I was finding myself overreacting every time there was chaos in my house. I realized that I should not be overreacting like this so I began to journal. I prayed and asked the Holy Spirit to reveal to me why I was acting this way. The Holy Spirit revealed the specific details of what had happened in my past, which allowed me to take these open wounds before the healing light of Jesus, and I healed. Again, I replaced the false belief/lie with the truth. "The heart is deceitful above all things and beyond cure. Who can understand it?" (Jer. 17:9).

Pray for God's truth to be revealed to you about what you remember if you are dealing with something in the past. God's truth about your bondage can lead to restoration. I'm a testimony that this is real. Notice that I asked the tough questions and the Lord answered and revealed to me things I would not have known. God is a God of restoration, and through the power of the cross, Jesus healed my broken emotions, and He will do the same for you.

So what did we learn? The Holy Spirit will reveal areas needing healing we might recognize as false statements, overreactions, trigger points, situations, and people who consume us. Journal and pray. Feel all feelings and share them with Jesus, opening up the wounds so His healing light can mend them. In the process, you may recognize areas needing attention such as bitterness, unforgiveness, lies and truth, and so forth. As you share all of your pain, open your wounds and allow Jesus to touch them, you will experience restoration.

The key to all of this is surrender! Once the Holy Spirit reveals an area needing healing, get out your journal. As you journal, write everything you can remember. And ask the Lord to help you remember things that you have forgotten. While the Lord may not reveal every single detail, He will reveal what you need to heal. Remember this is not about striving. The Holy Spirit will tell us things, but we must ask and then wait for the answer. Once you have journaled, cry, pray, and release all to Jesus, and ask Him to heal your wounds.

Jesus healed the wounds I experienced. He will do the same for you. He will walk with you as you face fears head-on. I had to face fear that made me feel I was experiencing what I most feared; however, when I faced it, I healed. I share this because the power of the blood of the cross is real and it brings healing. Jesus died for all of your present and past hurts. So take these hurts to the Lord, and allow Him to heal you. The Holy Spirit will guide you into all truth, and the truth will set you free. God did this for me on my journey, and He will do the same for you.

We talked about beauty from ashes. So in my example, it was as if God's glam truck showed up at my door to turn my ashes into beauty. You know what? I began to remember some good things from my childhood. When I completely surrendered it all, Jesus healed me. I no longer needed to control, my tough exterior softened, and my walls of self-protection came down.

To summarize, this is a process of getting head knowledge to heart knowledge, really getting it. When you get it that who you are in Christ does not change when things are done to you, that is, these things do not stick to you, there is joy. The healing comes from the process of realizing who you are in Christ (the dress/garment and nothing that happens to us defines us) + Holy Spirit revealing any lies that you may have made when you were hurt + the enemy lies being replaced with the truth (God's truth)

And ultimately sharing all of the pain and opening your wounds to the healing power of the blood of Jesus brings healing to your wounds.

Then the dress/garment/visual aid is further solidified for you. You will finally get it and believe it from your heart, not just your head.

Again, this is not an overnight, immediate process where we heal from all wounds at once. It is a process as we surrender to His leading (when he reveals the area needing healing). The power is released again by the work of Jesus Christ on the cross.

This afternoon as I was rushing to leave my house, I accidentally knocked my "Be Still and Know That He Is Always God" plaque off the counter, and it came tumbling onto the floor. As it did, I was reminded again that joy is not based on our circumstances. Also joy is never to be put on hold for a time when our circumstances change. It is deeper and spiritual. Because we know there is a day of deliverance, we want that in our timing. But we have to realize that God is sovereign, and in His perfect plan, all things will be made new. This may or may not be in this life. We have to be able to let go of the control.

And I lift my head and remember that day again. As I walked on the beach that afternoon, the Lord taught me that the joy is in Him. He revealed to me that He had been in all of the pain and He was using it for good. It was part of the big picture that we often cannot see. He allowed me to feel His love for me, His genuine concern about what I had suffered. He is a faithful, loving God. And suffering is part of His eternal plan. My prayer is that God will reveal this great joy to you. Remember, it is not based on human circumstances. Ask Him to show you the joy!

"Be still and Know that He is God" (Ps. 46:10). You see, there is always joy when there is hope. The joy comes from our hope, knowing that God will ultimately redeem everything, all the pain, all of it. Please do not miss the joy in the journey. Just like the silver sparkles on the beach, it is always right there. Please do not miss the joy in the journey as I did. You see, I was looking for the destination, and I lost sight of the journey. What I missed in retrospect was God being with me each step of the journey, all of the healing that happened along the way, and ultimately how God uses our suffering to help others.

Will you seek the joy in the journey and find it sooner than I did?

And once you find the joy, hold onto it and treasure it, for it is as sequins of hope in your journey to new life.

"Shout for joy to God, all the earth! Sing the glory of his name; make his praise glorious. Say to God, "How awesome are your deeds! So great is your power that your enemies cringe before you. All the earth bows down to you; they sing praise to you, they sing the praises of your" (Ps. 66:1–4).

Finally, I ask you, if you have never placed your trust in Christ, to do so today. Pray this prayer:

> Heavenly Father, I know that I am a sinner and I need a Savior. I believe that Jesus died for me and my sins and rose from the dead. I repent of my sins. Jesus, please come into my heart and journey with me as the leader of my life. I trust you, and I ask you to be the Lord and Savior of my life.

If you prayed that prayer from your heart, you have made the most important decision of your life, and you will spend eternity in heaven.

WORKS CITED

"New International Version." Accessed July 29, 2013. https://www.biblegateway.com.

"New Living Translation." Accessed July 29, 2013. https://www.biblegateway.com.

"Webster's 1913." http://www.websters1913.com.

ABOUT THE AUTHOR

Ally is a writer of hope. Her passion is to instill hope to the brokenhearted and to see lives changed. She has served the community in various outreach capacities. While serving as a minister of pastoral care, she received Holy Spirit inspired messages of hope and restoration which have been shared with those who were hurting. And, if that were not enough, her desire is to share the seeds of hope and healing that were planted in her – beginning as a small child - with whosoever will read these words.

Printed in the United States
By Bookmasters